The Employment and Information Law teams at Forbes Solicitors regularly advise a wide range of public and private sector organisations about law and practice affecting lone working. The team is involved in delivering briefings and providing training to managers and staff through shared sessions or in-house.

Their experience of advising and supporting of organisations, managing increased home and agile working in response to COVID-19 provides the basis for this book.

For more on Forbes Solicitors' information law work see their website at http://www.forbessolicitors.co.uk/business/business-law/gdpr.htm

For more on Forbes Solicitors' Employment work see their website at https://www.forbessolicitors.co.uk/business/employment.htm

Covid-19, Homeworking and the Law – The Essential Guide to Employment and GDPR Issues

Covid-19, Homeworking and the Law – The Essential Guide to Employment and GDPR Issues

Forbes Solicitors

Law Brief Publishing

Published 2020 by Law Brief Publishing, an imprint of Law Brief Publishing Ltd
30 The Parks
Minehead
Somerset
TA24 8BT

www.lawbriefpublishing.com

Paperback: 978-1-913715-08-3

PREFACE

In writing this book, we have set out to provide guidance to assist you with managing the employment and information law aspects of home and agile working in response to and as a consequence of Covid-19.

The style which we have adopted has been intended to assist someone with some prior basic knowledge of the relevant law to apply this knowledge but will hopefully also assist those getting to grips with these issues for the first time. We have included references throughout the book to the relevant parts of legislation, guidance and case law to assist the reader to consult with original source material if they want to undertake further reading into the subject.

This book is a collaborative effort from the Employment and Information Teams at Forbes Solicitors, with particular thanks to James Barron, Bethany Paliga and Daniel Milnes for writing the text and to Jonathan Holden for his support. We are also very grateful to Tim Kevan and Garry Wright for their encouragement in bringing this book into publication in record time.

The law in this book is that of England and Wales as stated at 30th June 2020 and this book should not be relied upon for the provision of, or as a substitute for, legal advice.

Forbes Solicitors
June 2020

CONTENTS

CHAPTER ONE
INTRODUCTION, SCOPE AND DEFINITIONS

The Covid-19 pandemic has produced dramatic effects in many aspects of life. In many businesses, charities and other organisations including government it has caused an unprecedented increase in the number of people working from home as a response to social distancing rules. The government required all those whose jobs could be done from home to work from home and at the time of writing that remains the case for a significant proportion of people with all indications pointing to greatly increased home and agile working numbers in future.

Employers are supporting home working as a Health and Safety measure to protect their staff and many are reviewing their requirements for office space with some announcing cost-saving office closures and moving to a partial or complete home or agile working model. Whether organisations act for one or both of those reasons the legal position remains the same and this book addresses two legal aspects of home and agile working which overlap very frequently: Data Protection and Employment.

Both areas of law are concerned with the management of change and the resulting risks and both involve assessment of how organisations should relate to their employees where there are onerous responsibilities for the organisation to discharge.

The specialist Information and Employment teams at Forbes have collaborated to produce this book as a general guide to how to get to grips with managing the Data Protection and Employment law aspects of home working in response to Covid-19.

Scope of This Book

This book sets out to provide practical commentary and guidance on aspects of the law as it applies to home and agile working in response to Covid-19.

The content addresses two principal topics:

a) Employment Law and some elements of related legal issues such as Health and Safety and

b) Data Protection under the GDPR and UK Data Protection Act 2018 with some commentary on the impact of the law on interception of communications.

Home working may engage other areas of law beyond the scope of this book, for example planning and insurance law as it applies to the use of buildings for permitted purposes and family law where there are consequences for domestic relationships. The relevant chapters indicate where these issues might arise and organisations or individuals should seek specialist advice if they do.

Terminology and Definitions

In the various chapters of this book we have used the terms commonly associated with the area of law to which the chapters relate.

Generally we have referred to "**home worker**" and "**home working**" to include those working from home, agile workers (those with no fixed place of work and who use different locations as work requires) and any combinations of the two including those working from home or in an agile way for some of the time and attending an office at other times.

In Part One the advice is addressed to employers and expressed as such referring to "the employer" or "**you**".

In Part Two we have referred to "the organisation" to include a range of legal entities and to reflect that in relation to Information Law compliance the positions and actions of other legal entities will also be of interest and relevance. We have included references to "data controller" or "controller" using the terms as defined in the GDPR.

Some abbreviations and references are used throughout the book for convenience and they are:

ACAS	Advisory Conciliation and Arbitration Service
BYOD	Bring Your Own Device
Data Protection Act	Data Protection Act 2018
DPIA	Data Protection Impact Assessment
ECJ	European Court of Justice (Court of Justice of the European Union)
EDPB	European Data Protection Board (formerly Article 29 Working Party)
ERA	Employment Rights Act 1996
Equality Act	Equality Act 2010
Flexible Working Regulations	The Flexible Working Regulations 2014
GDPR	General Data Protection Regulation (Regulation (EU) 2016/679)
ICO	Information Commissioner's Office
IPA	Investigatory Powers Act 2016
IP Regulations	The Investigatory Powers (Interception by Businesses etc. for Monitoring and Record-keeping Purposes) Regulations 2018

National Minimum Wage Regulations	The National Minimum Wage Regulations 2015
TULRCA	Trade Union and Labour Relations (Consolidation) Act 1992
Working Time Regulations	The Working Time Regulations 1998

CHAPTER TWO
WHY CONSIDER HOMEWORKING?

The evolution of home working

The phrase "home working" has no strict definition in UK employment law legislation. It can cover a wide range of situations ranging from employees who have asked to work from home for a single day to wait in for a delivery or tradesperson, to an employee who has asked to work from home for a day a week to an employee who never attends the office and their place of work is their home.

A study by the Office for National Statistics showed that in 2019 1.7 million people reported that they predominantly worked from home, with 8.7 million people reporting they sometimes worked from home. That 8.7 million number roughly represents 30% of the UK workforce and 1.7 million people represents just over 5% of the UK workforce.

These are large numbers and these numbers have been steadily growing, increasing from 4.3% of the workforce in 2015 to 5.1% of the workforce in 2019. This increase has largely been possible thanks to advancements in technology making home working easier but with the outbreak of Covid-19 it seems reasonable to assume with large numbers of people having to work from home and employers and employees seeing its benefits, that these numbers will only get higher.

Whilst certainly it is the case that not all roles are suitable for home working most employers are likely to have employees who can do their job from home and so home working is something that all employers should consider. Using manufacturing as an example, those working on the "shop-floor" are unlikely to have roles that can be done from home, but those working in finance or HR functions may be able to.

Types of home working

As stated above there is no strict legal definition of home working but broadly home working can be broken down into 3 categories.

Situational – In this category is employees who will work predominantly work in an office environment but in certain situations may work from home. This may include employees working from home to be around for a delivery etc. These will only be occasional instances and only in certain circumstances.

Regular – These are employees who regularly work from home but also work in the office. A common term given to employees in these situations is agile workers, i.e. those who have the flexibility to choose where the best location for them to carry out their work in any given day whether that be at home or in an office.

Permanent – These are employees whose permanent place of work is their home address and working from home is the norm and attending an office is an exception.

What are the benefits to an employee at working from home?

Generally the reason employees wish to work from home is the added flexibility that comes from home working along with allowing work to fit into their lives. It is common for employees to request home working to allow them to take their children to school or allow them to carry out household tasks whilst also working, which is not possible in a working environment.

The key benefit though that most employees would identify is the ability to avoid their commute into work and the associated costs involved with that.

Benefits for employers

Often when considering home working the benefits to the employee is the primary thing which is considered but there can be considerable benefits to the employer.

Firstly, having a large number of your workforce not working in offices can significantly reduce the need for costly office space and the associated overheads. As an example, in 2009 IBM through encouraging home working were able to encourage 40% of their staff to work from home saving them an estimated $2 billion as a result of offloading office space which was no longer needed.

Home working is also popular with employees and employees often report feeling more productive due to the lack of commute and the increased satisfaction that they have when working from home. Obviously happier and more productive employees are good for employers.

It can also be a fantastic tool in allowing employers to attract and retain the best talent for their organisation. Home working is often seen as a good indicator of a work life balance which employees are favouring in greater numbers so it can allow them to attract and retain the best talent. Additionally, it can widen the pool of employees they can look for, if employees would be reluctant to commute long distances to an employer's office allowing those employees to work from home can entice employees to consider that opportunity.

Finally, it is also a much more environmentally friendly way of carrying out business with the large number of trips to the office it prevents and can form part of an organisation's Corporate Social Responsibility policy.

What are the downsides for home working?

As has been seen during the Covid-19 outbreak, some employees have expressed weariness from the increased home working. The nature of home working means that it can be relatively solitary and so steps need to be taken by an employer to ensure the wellbeing of their staff and this is harder when there is not necessarily daily contact with these employees.

Some people feel that working from home can also stifle creativity without the constant contact with colleagues and new ideas that can come from that collaboration. A good example of this is IBM, despite saving an estimated $2 billion by having large numbers of the workforce working from home in 2017 they massively scaled back their home working complaining how it had stifled creativity and innovation in the workplace and required large numbers of their home workers to now work in an office environment.

Finally, home working can be more difficult for employers to manage due to the lack of day to day control. As such a high degree of trust is required between the parties.

What impact will Covid-19 have on home working?

It is expected that Covid-19 will have a significant increase in home working with far larger numbers likely to see home working as an option having carried out home working for significant periods of 2020.

One issue that employers might find going forward as a result though is that home working has to an extent been normalised. Previously home working has been seen as a perk that only some employers offered but with it becoming normalised the value that employees place on home working may diminish. This in turn may impact employers as prior to Covid-19 an employee was likely to see home working as a significant perk and with it becoming more normalised employers may need to consider other forms of reward or offer more generous home working terms to account for this.

Employers also might find it harder to turn down home working requests in the future. Currently employers have wide discretion to turn down home working requests but having had significant numbers of staff working from home for significant periods of time justifying turning down a request may be harder in the future.

Finally, as a result of Covid-19 we may reassess our view on home working. There is currently a right to request flexible working, which includes home working, within UK law but there is no formal right to work from home. With the extended number of people who have been working at home for significant periods this attitude may change in the future.

CHAPTER THREE
DEALING WITH A REQUEST TO WORK FROM HOME – FORMAL FLEXIBLE WORKING REQUESTS

Introduction

As a result of the situation with Covid-19 large parts of the UK working population ended up working from home out of necessity without having made any request to do so. This is not traditionally the case though as ordinarily an employee wishing to work from home would need to make a request to their employer to work from home.

Covid-19 has shown many employers and employees that working from home can be possible and the benefits of doing so but employers need to be aware of how to deal with requests to work from home in a fair and consistent manner which does not fall foul of employment law legislation.

Formal Flexible Working Request

At this moment in time, there is no technical right within UK employment law legislation which gives an employee the right to work from home.

However, since 2014 and the passing of the *Flexible Working Regulations* there has been provision within the ERA.

The section which covers flexible working requests can be found at s.80F of the ERA. This gives employees the power to request changes to their terms of employment if the changes relate to either:

1. The hours they work;
2. The time they are required to work; or
3. Where they are required to work.

It is the third option here which gives the employees the right to make a formal request for home working under these provisions.

ACAS has also produced useful guidance for employers in dealing with flexible working requests. Whilst the ACAS code is not binding on employers it does provide guidance on best practice and should be followed as far as is possible.

One thing that should be noted for employers and employees is that the effect of an employee making a request under s.80F of the ERA is that it makes a change, a permanent one, to their terms and conditions of employment. Therefore whilst technically an employee could make a request under s.80F on a temporary basis ordinarily temporary requests are best not considered through the formal flexible working route due to this formal change in the contract of employment and are best done through other means which are considered in Chapter 4.

Who is eligible to make a flexible working request?

Not everyone who works for a business is eligible to make a request for flexible working under s.80F of the ERA. Only those members of staff who meet certain criteria may be eligible to make such a request.

There are 4 tests someone must meet to be eligible to make a request under s.80F of the ERA.

1. The person making the request must be an employee

The scope of the status of a member of staff within an organisation is outside the scope of this book, but in brief terms at this time there are essentially 3 categories of people who may work for an organisation. You have employees, workers, and self-employed members of staff.

There are a number of tests which can be carried out on a member of staff's working situation to determine their status but the key reason this is often important is that employees have far more protection in UK employment law legislation that workers or those who are self-employed.

A flexible working request is an example of this, so only employees of an organisation have a right to make a flexible working request, not worker or self-employed individuals.

2. They must have at least 26 week's continuous service

An employee will need to have had 26 week's continuous service before they can make a flexible working application under s.80F. This 26 week's continuous service requirement therefore gives employers some protection that a new employee cannot make a request immediately upon starting with an employer. This is particular helpful in the context of home working where you may need any employee to work in the office for a period of time until they are acclimatised to an employer's systems and are able to work from home.

It is important to note that is continuous service rather than how long they have been employed with the organisation. This means that if the employee has been subject to a TUPE transfer into the organisation or has come from to that organisation where previous service is recognised, then service with their previous employer would need to be taken into account as well.

3. They must have not made a request under s.80F of the ERA in the past 12 months

Employees can only make a request every 12 months. This prevents employees from seeking to abuse the system by making frequent requests from their employer if one has been previously turned down.

4. They must not be in a category excluded from making a request under s.80F

There are broadly speaking 3 groups of people excluded from making a flexible working request. These include members of the armed forces and employee shareholders, however for the majority of organisations these two excluded categories are not relevant.

One area which might be relevant for most organisations though is that the right to request flexible working under s.80(F) does not apply to agency workers.

Both agency workers and employee shareholders do have a limited right to make an application for flexible working under s.80F but only in respect of those who are returning from a period of parental leave.

Process for dealing with a request

When making an application for flexible working, s.80F and the Flexible Working Regulations provide some elements that an application for flexible working needs to include if it is to be a valid.
It must:

- Be in writing;
- State that it is an application under s.80F of the ERA;
- Be dated;

- State the change they are requesting and when they wish the change to take effect;
- State if the employee has made an application for flexible working and if so when; and
- Explain the effect that the change will have on the employer and how the employee thinks that effect might be dealt with.

The ACAS Code on Flexible Working also suggests that requests should also make clear if their request is due to a protected characteristic under the Equality Act, such as for caring purposes or health reasons.

The easiest way of ensuring all this information is included in a request is by an employer including a specified form with the details they need to fill out and some explanation.

In particular employees should be encouraged as far as possible to consider the effect of the change and how this might be mitigated. This requirement can be very useful from the perspective of an employer as it makes the employee properly think how the impact might be mitigated and those flexible working requests which include detailed information here are the ones that are more likely to be granted.

Under s.80G(1) of the ERA it makes clear that an employer should deal with any flexible working application in a reasonable manner. The legislation doesn't specify what is meant by "a reasonable manner", however the ACAS Code on Flexible Working does provide some guidance for employees which if followed is likely to show that the application was dealt with in a reasonable manner.

The first step upon receipt of a request for home working under this procedure therefore would be for an employer to arrange to meet with the employee to discuss their request as soon as possible, the only exception to this would be if the employer intends to grant the request in any event.

In these discussions the employer should be clear about what changes the employee is requesting and the practical effect they see happening from those changes, such as if they have supervisory responsibilities. The employer should also make clear if the home working is going to cause any impact on benefits that they have and make sure the employee is aware of this.

There is no strict legal requirement for an employer to allow an employee to be accompanied to these meetings but it would be best practice and is recommended by the ACAS Code that employees are allowed to bring either a colleague or a Trade Union representative to this meeting to discuss the proposals.

An employer should also make clear from the outset the expected timescales they require to come to a decision to manage the expectations of the employee, particularly as the timescales for an employer to come to a decision are particularly long.

If an employee fails to attend this arranged meeting to discuss their request without good reason on two separate occasions then the employer can treat the application for flexible working as being withdrawn and the employee will then not be able to make another request for 12 months.

Coming to a decision

S.80G of the ERA sets out the timescales in which an employer needs to have made a determination on the employee's request, which is 3 months from the date the employee made the request. This is the date at which the formal request is made so if an employee discussed making an application for home working using the statutory regime then the 3 months start from when they formally made their application. As the majority of applications are sent electronically or hand delivered, it should be relatively obvious in most circumstances when the 3-month deadline will pass.

An employer and employee can also agree to extend this 3-month period but there needs to be agreement between the parties. In practice most employees will often agree to any extension as extensions are only generally necessary if the employer needs additional time to consider the request and due to the relative wide flexibility they have to deny a request it is often in the best interests of the employee to give the employer as much time as possible to consider the request.

Granting a request

If the employer grants the employee's request then the home working requested by the employee will form a permanent change to the employee's terms of employment.

If the employee is going to work from home on a full time basis or predominantly work from home it is likely that their place of work will have changed and this information is part of the information that is required to be included in an employee's particulars of employment under s.1 of the ERA.

Under s.4 of the ERA if there are any changes which are made to an employee's particulars of employment, they need to be given a new statement of particulars of employment within at least one month of the change happening.

As an employer is required to make these changes under s.4 of the ERA in any event and issue a new contract of employment it would be sensible for an employer to consider the rest of the contract and any new contractual terms they may wish to include within the contract. Chapter 7 includes key points on what contractual terms should be considered within the contract of a home worker.

As well as the legal requirements it is also good practice to have regular reviews with the employee once home working has been implemented so both parties can discuss how it is working and if necessary if any changes are required to the initial agreements that were made.

Refusing a request

Under the statutory flexible working request scheme if an employer is going to refuse an employee's request for flexible working then it needs to rely on one of eight reasons set out at s.80G of the ERA, these are:

- The burden of additional costs.
- Detrimental effect on ability to meet customer demand.
- Inability to reorganise work among existing staff.
- Inability to recruit additional staff.
- Detrimental impact on quality.
- Detrimental impact on performance.
- Insufficiency of work during the periods the employee proposes to work.
- Planned structural changes.

The test is a subjective one for the employer to determine and so if the employer considers that any of these eight reasons apply then it can refuse the request.

There is no legal requirement to give an explanation on why the employer considers one of these particular statutory reasons to refuse the request is applicable in the circumstances. However, it is best practice to provide an explanation as there can be potential consequences if an employer refuses a request and so providing an explanation on the refusal should be considered.

In practice with the wide ranging reasons that an employer can refuse a request and the fact that it is the employer's subjective decision means that in practice in most circumstances an employer will be able to justify refusing most requests for flexible working if they don't feel they are workable.

Appeals

Technically there is no statutory requirement for an employer to allow an employee a right of appeal against a decision to refuse a flexible working request. However the ACAS Code recommends that employers offer one and an appeal can be a good opportunity for an employer to consider its original decision and it makes it more likely that an employer will have dealt with the application in a reasonable manner.

If an employer does grant an employee a right of appeal it should try as far as possible to try and follow the ordinary procedural elements that they would consider in any appeal process. This includes having a more senior member of staff hearing the appeal than the person who made the initial decision and ensuring the person hearing the appeal has had no involvement in the original decision-making process.

What issues might employers face if they refuse a request?

As seen earlier in this Chapter the circumstances in which an employer can refuse an employee's flexible working request are very wide. Realistically these options are wide enough that an employer can reject the majority of applications for one of these reasons.

An employee can technically bring a claim against their employer for a failure to properly consider a request for flexible working under s.80F of the ERA but such claims are very rare for a few reasons.

Firstly, the circumstances in which an employee can bring a claim are quite limited and are primarily due to failings in the process rather than any actual decision. These circumstances are:

- The employer failed to deal with the request in a reasonable manner,
- The employer did not deal with the request within the require time frame;
- The employer rejected the claim for a reason other than those set out in the statute;
- The employer's decision was based on incorrect facts; or
- The employer considered the request withdrawn when it was not entitled to do so.

The other reason these claims are rare is that the remedies available to employees are fairly limited. An Employment Tribunal has two options open to it in these claims, and it can choose to award one or both of them.

The Tribunal can ask for the employer to reconsider the request. The employment Tribunal importantly does not have the power to substitute its own decision for that of the employer. Therefore, it is open to the employer even upon an order for reconsideration to still come to the same decision it did in the first instance.

A Tribunal can also award compensation but the amounts again are limited. A Tribunal can award up to eight week's pay to an employee in circumstances where it brings a successful claim for a breach of s.80F of the ERA but that pay is limited to a set statutory amount. As such the maximum an employee could be awarded between 6th April 2020 and 5th April 2021 is £4304.

Whilst claims for an actual breach of the s.80F of the ERA are rare by themselves a failure to grant a request from an employee may result in other claims being brought against an employer.

A rejection of a flexible working request could result in a claim from an employee of constructive dismissal. An employee could claim that their employer acted in such an unreasonable manner when considering their flexible working request that it has destroyed the trust and confidence between the parties. In all likelihood for such a claim to be successful the employer would have had to have acted in a particularly unreasonable manner and a simple rejection of their request would be insufficient.

The most likely claim an employer may receive for refusing a request to work from home from an employee is likely to be a potential discrimination claim and these circumstances are dealt with in more detail in Chapter 4.

CHAPTER FOUR
DEALING WITH A REQUEST TO WORK FROM HOME – CONSIDERING REQUESTS OUTSIDE OF THE STATUTORY REGIME

Introduction

In Chapter 3 we have dealt with the legal process by which employees can make a request for flexible working arrangements which include home working.

The statutory regime only provides a minimum requirement though and as it is not designed solely for home working, employers may choose to go above these statutory requirements and design a system which is more focused around the issues surrounding home working.

The most effective means of doing this is through a home working policy and this Chapter considers why an employer may wish to have a home working policy as well as some of the things they may wish to include in such a policy. This Chapter will fill in some of the advantages that a home working policy may give an employer over relying on the statutory flexible working regime. More details around what sort of information should be included in a home working policy along with changes to employee's contracts that should be considered can be found in Chapter 7.

The primary advantage a home working policy has over any other means is the control it gives the employer to set the parameters of what they will allow in a home working environment.

Temporary home working requests

For some employees home working is a permanent solution – they want to consider to work either predominantly or solely at home. For others however this may be a temporary solution to deal with unexpected or difficult circumstances where home working for a short period of time is likely to be beneficial to them. This is the situation that we have found ourselves in with Covid-19, this is not a formal change to everyone's working patterns it is at least in principle a temporary change to everyone's normal working location to try and minimise contact with others and minimise the spread of the disease.

Whilst Covid-19 is an extreme example of a temporary home working situation there are likely to be other every-day situations where an employee may require to work from home for a period which might range from a few hours to a few weeks, these include:

- Waiting at home for a tradesperson or delivery;
- Disruption in child or other care arrangements;
- After a period of paternity leave to ease the transition back to work;
- Disruption to public transport networks whether due to industrial action or extreme weather;
- Following an injury which makes travel and working in an office environment difficult, such as a broken leg; or
- When working on a particular project where quiet uninterrupted time is likely to be beneficial.

A request using the statutory scheme under s.80F of the ERA can technically be used for temporary requests as there is no prohibition on it being considered in that way. However, it is not necessarily the best way of dealing with temporary requests as it is intention of the legislation is to create a permanent change to the employee's terms and conditions.

It also creates problems: if people are using the opportunity to work from home an ad-hoc basis: the requirement that requests can only be made once in a twelve month period would make the scheme un-workable and the time scales involved with the formal system may mean the reason to request home working in the first place has dissipated.

It is therefore preferable for employers to have a dedicated home working policy rather to allow employees to make temporary requests rather than just relying upon the statutory regime.

A home working policy can have a set system for an employee to request working from home in these circumstances whether that is simply by discussing their request to work from home with their manager or other more formal means. Employers may want to determine if employees need to be "pre-approved" to work from home before they can work from home and a policy can deal with this.

What additional information can be considered as part of a request through a home working policy

One of the primary advantage of a specific home working policy is that you can be much more focused in the information you require to make a decision rather than relying on generic responsibilities employers may have under the statutory flexible working request provisions of s.80F of the ERA and it can be tailored to the needs of an individual employer.

Additionally, you can manage the expectations of employees and make clear the circumstances where you are unlikely to grant home working on a permanent basis, whether this be due to demands of the role or concerns about performance. This can be set out in the policy and it can make employees aware that they are unlikely to be granted home working before they apply and prevent both parties having to go through a process which is unlikely to be successful.

You can also make clear the behaviours and skills you will expect from employees who will work at home within a policy. Each employer will have different requirements for its employees to be able to work from home so an employer can tailor their home working policy to make clear the behaviours they would expect from an employee. Again, this has the advantage of managing the expectations of any employees so they are aware of what is required of them before making a home working request.

Employers can also be far more detailed when they are considering a home working request about the sort of information they will need from an employee to help them make a decision whether or not to grant the request. If the employer wants to ensure that all those staff members working meet certain criteria it can set out those criteria and ask the employee to determine how they meet the criteria.

A home working policy is useful for setting out the expectations you have as an employer and to ask the employee to proactively address those issues and how they will be overcome. So for instance an employer may ask how they foresee supervision taking place, how their role would suit a home working environment and whether they would have any degree of flexibility if they were required in the office for a particular reason. The advantage for an employer in asking this information is that home working requires a degree of initiative and self-motivation, by giving an employee the framework in which a decision will be made it is common to treat their response as somewhat of a test to see if they are suitable to be able to work from home.

Technically speaking if a request is considered through a home working policy an employer doesn't need to follow the same process as they would through a statutory flexible working request however the provisions of the ACAS Code on flexible working does set out a sensible procedure that is not too onerous on an employer and therefore it can make sense if same process is replicated in the home working policy.

Additionally, when considering a request through a flexible working scheme if the employer chooses to reject the request there is no requirement that this is done for one of the reasons found at s.80F of the ERA. Employers could choose to set out the factors they will consider in coming to a decision within a home working policy to ensure there is full transparency over the decisions or instead could be silent on this to ensure they have as much flexibility as possible when coming to a decision, this is a decision for an employer to consider what is more important for them in a home working policy.

Trial periods

One key thing which parties can consider when dealing with a home working request is to implement a trial period before coming to a permanent decision.

The employer and employee can agree a period of time between them to trial the working arrangements with both parties considering whether the working arrangement is sustainable as a long-term arrangement.

Trial periods often work well and in the majority of cases it is likely to be more reasonable for an employer to suggest a trial period for a home working request to see whether any concerns they may have about granting the request are valid before deciding whether or not to grant any request.

Trial periods may not be suitable in all circumstances though, particularly if the employee requires significant specific equipment to enable home working, but in most circumstances can be useful for both parties.

What issues might employers face if they refuse a request?

In this Chapter we have looked at dealing with requests that are made via a home working policy and as such there is not going to be a specific claim an employee could bring if they believe their request has been unfairly refused.

Again an employee could make a claim for constructive dismissal but provided the employer has a reasonable reason for refusing the request and has dealt with the request in a fair way it is likely that they would have a strong defence against such claims.

If, which would be very unusual, an employer had a contractual home working policy then a failure to follow this process properly could result in a claim in respect of a breach of contract but these circumstances would be very rare and it would be difficult for an employee to show what their losses would be in these circumstances.

The most claim an employer is likely to face for a rejection of a request for home working, however it has been requested, is a discrimination claim.

There may be some circumstances where a refusal to allow a request for home working may give rise to a direct discrimination claim. If an employee can show that a comparator employee had been previously been allowed to work from home and their request had been refused then this may lead to a claim for direct discrimination. Particular care should therefore be taken when dealing with competing requests for flexible working and this issue is explored further in Chapter 8.

In general women seek flexible working arrangements such as home working in higher numbers than men, therefore a failure to consider a flexible working request may be an act of indirect sex discrimination. Employers have a defence against any indirect discrimination cases if they can show their actions where a proportionate means of achieving a legitimate aim. Therefore, it is important that when taking any decision to refuse a flexible working request there is a clear rationale for this reason and this reason is recorded. This will help the employer defend against any claims that an employee may bring in this respect to show they had a legitimate aim and properly considered the circumstances of the employee and acted in a fair way to show that their decision taken was a proportionate one.

Employers should also be cautious when considering the performance of employees during the Covid-19 situation when determining whether or not to allow them to work from home. The Covid-19 situation is an extreme one whereby all normally available childcare options are unavailable to parents. Studies have shown that women have taken a higher burden of the domestic responsibility including home schooling children during the period where they are working from home due to Covid-19. Therefore if an employer were to turn down a request to work from home on the basis of a lack of productivity during the Covid-19 period, again this could be a form of indirect sex discrimination and employers should therefore be cautious about attaching too much weight to performance during the Covid-19 situation.

Another key claim that could arise from a failure to grant a home working request is whether granting home working would be a reasonable adjustment for a disabled employee and indeed most of the reported employment law cases on home working are around reasonable adjustments.

A common disability which might require an employee to consider home working is agoraphobia and there have been a couple of reported cases [1]These cases and the differing decisions reached in them are useful examples of the situations employers should be wary of in circumstances which may amount to disability discrimination.

---

1 *British Communications v Miss Lynn Pelling EATS/0093/03* and *The Secretary of State for Work and Pensions (Job Centre Plus) and Others v Ms J Wilson UKEAT/0289/09/DA.*

In the first case Ms Pelling suffered from agoraphobia and was eventually dismissed by reason of capability. Ms Pelling's employer had tried to deal with her situation as sensitively as possible but at no stage during the process did they consider home working as an alternative to dismissal, although this was never raised by Ms Pelling or her union representative during the dismissal process a tribunal found that by the employer not considering this, that her dismissal was unfair and discriminatory. The Employment Appeal Tribunal took account that Ms Pelling's employer had large numbers of people who were working from home and so the possibility of home working should have occurred to them and been considered.

This case can be contrasted with the second case, where Ms Wilson's office close to where she lived had closed and she then claimed that the failure to allow her to work from home was an act of disability discrimination. In this case the Employment Appeal Tribunal had took account of the detailed consideration the employer had of the employee's request before determining it was not feasible and the other alternatives the employer considered such as providing a taxi or providing a colleague or support worker to take her to the new offices, which were all rejected by the employee. The Employment Appeal Tribunal determined that it was not feasible for the employee to work from home and therefore allowing her to do so was not a reasonable adjustment.

Finally, whilst using a home working policy allows an employer to set out its expectations on what they require from home workers they should ensure that those requirements do not indirectly discriminate against disabled employees. If for instance an employer required certain levels of productivity to allow an employee to work from home this could lead to a claim of indirect discrimination unless the employer can show that this policy was a proportionate means of achieving a legitimate aim. Similarly if an employer has concerns around an employee's performance but the performance is caused by a disability then this can cause difficulties and employers will need to consider what their reasons are for not allowing that employee to work from home and whether the refusal of home working is a proportionate means of achieving that reason.

CHAPTER FIVE
SUPERVISION AND MANAGEMENT OF HOMEWORKERS

Introduction

Home workers present a unique challenge for employers in respect of their management and supervision. Unlike workers who are working in offices it can be difficult to accurately monitor employees who are not working in an office with other staff members present.

A lot of home working comes down to trust between the employee and the employer and as such it is common in many home working policies to prevent employees from making use of such a policy until they have passed their probationary period so the employer has some degree of trust in their performance levels before they start home working.

How to measure the performance of home workers

Different organisations have different ways in which they can measure the productivity of their employees and some are more suited to home working than others. As an example, solicitors traditionally record working time in 6 minute units, a firm of solicitors could analyse how many units a particular solicitor is recording whilst working from home compared to whilst working in an office to make a determination on the productivity of that employee.

Therefore, it is important before an employer considers granting an employee's request to work from home that they consider how they can measure if the employee is working effectively. In some circumstances, such as the example of solicitors above, objective measures can be made but in other industries it is likely to be to an extent subjective and based partially at least, on the home worker's manager's assessment of the employee's performance.

Therefore, provisions should be put in place to ensure that managers of home workers are properly supervising these employees. Often this can be done by ensuring there are more regular catch-up meetings between home workers and their managers than would ordinarily happen in an office environment where an employer would have a higher degree of control. This can also have the added benefit of working to ensure the wellbeing of the home working employee.

Building upon these regular catch-ups it can also be useful to ensure that regular appraisals take place so both parties have a means of feeding back any issues they may have with home working and addressing any performance concerns.

There can be more invasive means of monitoring employee's performance such as through the use of employee monitoring software, but employers should be aware of the potential consequences this may have from a data protection perspective. This is addressed in Chapter 15.

Making use of a home working policy

A home working policy should set out expectations that employers have for employees in respect of their performance and the consequences if their performance is not at a sufficient level.

Home workers are subject to the same obligations that any other employee of an employer would have and therefore if an employer has concerns about performance then there would be nothing preventing them from carrying out a performance management process to improve the employee's performance.

This is another occasion where have a home working policy in place can be really beneficial. It is common within a home working policy to include a clause which ensures that if the employer has concerns regarding the employee's performance they can remove their ability to work from home and instead require them to come into the office. This should make any performance management process easier and more effective.

If it is not possible for whatever reason for the employer to require the employee to attend an office following concerns about their performance then the employer should treat the situation the same as any other performance management process but think about how the employee's performance can be monitored and how and where meetings will take place.

If there will be monitoring, setting out what it will be and why it will happen in the home working policy can address the GDPR requirements for transparency and notices of processing.[1]

Ensuring the wellbeing of the employee

It is important to note that for an employer that an employee working from home is still an employee and therefore they should be treated in a similar manner to other employees employed by the employer.

The home workers manager should also do as much as possible to ensure the employee working from home feels part of the employer's business. A key oversight that can happen for employees who solely work from home is employers forgetting to invite them to work social events, including the Christmas party. Therefore, efforts should be made to include them.

1 GDPR Article 5 (1) (a) and Article 13.

Many employees are using video conferencing as an alternative to in-person meetings. The data protection issues that can arise are addressed in Chapter 14.

On a day to day basis the employee's manager should engage with the employee to determine how much contact they want outside of supervision and management to keep them feeling part of the team.

Employers should also consider the benefits that those working in the office have and whether it is practical to extend those benefits to home working employees. Examples of this could be on site gyms or a subsidised onsite canteen, if you have staff who work from home should allowances be made to ensure these staff can still access these benefits. There is no technical legal obligation on an employer to ensure these benefits are available for all staff but from a wellbeing perspective employers should be wary of this.

Due to an employer's obligations in respect of health and safety they should strongly consider providing their own specialised equipment to those who work from home on a permanent basis to minimise the risk as far as is possible.

CHAPTER SIX
INTERACTION OF HOMEWORKING WITH OTHER ELEMENTS OF EMPLOYMENT LAW

Introduction

Home workers are much like any other employees and they consequently have the same rights under employment legislation as any other employee would have.

However the very nature of them working from home means that there are certain issues that become slightly more complex when dealing with those who work from home.

Disciplinary and Grievance processes for home workers

Due to the sudden nature of offices closing during the Covid-19 outbreak a common issue that needed to be dealt with was what would happen with any disciplinary or grievance process that was ongoing.

ACAS did eventually release guidance on this point and this guidance was perhaps a bit conservative in that it did suggest that depending on the circumstances employers should wait until a return to the office to deal with issues but this was not strictly necessary as there is no legal requirement that disciplinary or grievance proceedings take place face to face and it would be unusual for such a requirement to be in an employer's disciplinary policy.

However in more ordinary circumstances these issues are not too much of a concern for employers and the only thing they likely need to consider is the location of any disciplinary or grievance meetings as whilst they can be done remotely it is more efficient and best for both parties if they take place as face to face hearings.

It would normally make sense to include provisions requiring the employee to attend one of an employer's offices to cover events such as these but there may be circumstances, such as if there is a large distance between the employer's location and the employee's home address where neutral venues need to be considered.

When considering neutral venues, employers should be mindful of the employee's right to confidentiality and so public spaces such as coffee shops or motorway service stations would rarely be appropriate and employers should instead look to hire office space on a daily basis to carry out these meetings.

Other than the location all other aspects of a disciplinary or grievance hearing for office workers would be the same for home workers. One thing an employer should consider is the employee's right to be accompanied to a meeting and considering the geographic distance between an employee and their choice of companion, thought should be given to the practicalities of the companion attending in these circumstances.

Collective Consultations and home workers

Section.188 of TULRCA requires that employers who are proposing to dismiss as redundant more than 20 employees at one establishment within a 90-day period have to carry out a minimum period of consultation with the affected employees.

One question that is often considered is what is the meaning of the word "establishment" within TULRCA and how would this impact on home workers?

The issue on the definition of an establishment was the subject of an ECJ case, [1]which is colloquially known as the "Woolworths case". The case came about following Woolworths going into administration which resulted in large scale redundancies and the required period of information and consultation did not take place. When these claims were considered at Employment Tribunal, taking the ordinary meaning of the word "establishment" the Tribunals only awarded compensation for employees who had worked in stores where more than 20 redundancies took place.

As mentioned earlier this case went all the way to the ECJ and they set out guidance on how an "establishment" should be interpreted and effectively this is in a very broad way and of particular significance for home workers is that geographical issues are not necessarily of significance.

Therefore employers if they are carrying out a redundancy exercise will need to consider whether home workers form part of an "establishment" predominantly by looking at the work they carry out, the teams they are part of and the management structure they fall under to determine whether they will form part of an establishment for the purposes of TULRCA and whether they should be included for the purposes of any collective consultation.

If there is any ambiguity, considering the serious consequences for an employer of failing in its information and consultation obligations under TULRCA (each affected employee would be entitled to 13 weeks' pay), it may choose to be cautious in its approach of including them within an establishment.

---

1 *USDAW v WW Realisation 1 Ltd. Case C-80/14*

Interaction between home working and TUPE

If there is a whole business sale, then the employee will clearly transfer to the new employer as part of that sale. All parties will have to think about what they do to include home workers as part of the consultation process but considering the extended use of video meeting platforms as a result of home working caused by Covid-19 then this should be possible to facilitate if employees are unable to come into the office as part of a consultation. See Chapter 14 for more on the use of video conferencing especially where confidential matters are being discussed.

What can be slightly more complicated is in circumstances such as a service provision change or a transfer of part of a business and whether a home worker would be part of the "organised grouping" who would be part of the transfer.

What constitutes an organised grouping of employee is relatively wide and geography doesn't necessarily factor into determining this. Instead employers should look at the work that individuals carry out to determine that organised grouping and home workers may fall into that category and may therefore have their employment transferred under TUPE.

Working Time issues for home workers

One key difficulty with employees working from home is the lack of control that an employer has over an employee who is working from home. Whilst this can manifest in difficulties in respect of lack of supervision and performance issues it can also be common that employees who work from home can often struggle to draw clear distinctions between their work and home life. This needs to be managed for an employee welfare perspective and this is covered in Chapter 5, but employers should also be aware of their obligations under the Working Time Regulations and National Minimum Wage obligations.

As employers lack control over the employees there need to remind their employees of how much time they need to spend not working under the Working Time Regulations, the key issues which can cause issues for employers with home workers are:

- The 48-hour maximum working week;
- The requirement for a 20-minute break if working for more than 6 hours; and
- Uninterrupted rest period of 11 hours.

Employers need to be careful in respect of Working Time Regulations obligations as the consequences for employers can be relatively severe if they breach these obligations. Employers may think that if employees are breaching their own Working Time Regulation rest periods it is unlikely they will bring a claim. Whilst this may be true in practice, Working Time breaches can be prosecuted by local authorities and the Health and Safety Executive and can result in fines for employers who are found to be in breach.

In practice to try and alleviate these issues employers should ensure that employees are aware of the breaks they are entitled to and as far as possible make sure these breaks are taken. This could be by inserting clauses into any contract making clear they will abide by all required rest they should taking under the Working Time Regulations or setting this out in a policy. Employers may also choose to ask all employees working from home to sign an opt out of the 48-hour working week to ensure they have protection if their home working employees work for longer than 48 hours.

A distinction can be made though between employees who are working from home to fulfil the duties they would ordinarily fulfil and those who choose to work from home voluntarily, for example an employee who is taking work home to finish in their own time. This time is generally not counted as working time and so employers should not be too concerned that they may be in breach of the Working Time Regulations if they allow employees to do this.

One key issue that can arise with home workers is the status of travelling time in respect of the Working Time Regulations. For employees whose place of work is their home address and therefore have no fixed office, then for the purposes of the Working Time Regulations the travel to their first job of the day and the travel back from their last job of the day should be classed as working time[2]. Therefore employers who have home workers whose work involves them travelling to either different sites or to client premises they should be wary that the travelling time between jobs needs to be considered for Working Time purposes.

National Minimum Wage Issues

Similarly to concerns regarding the Working Time Regulations, employers should also be conscious about the amount of hours a home worker is carrying out for the purposes of calculating their pay for the purposes of the National Minimum Wage.

An employer can find itself in difficulty if they have an employee who is paid at the National Minimum Wage level or just above National Minimum Wage if they work significantly in excess of their contracted hours as this may result in the employee's remuneration dropping below the National Minimum Wage.

Considering the tough enforcement action that an employer may find itself subject to for breaches of the National Minimum Wage Regulations employers should consider what action they can take to ensure that no breaches take place. This may mean in practice that employers may have to consider whether they will only consider allowing home

---

2 *Federacion de Servicios Privados del sindicato Comisiones obreras v Tyco Integrated Security SL (Case C-266/14) [2015] IRLR 935*

working to employees who have a salary at a level to ensure there are no concerns in respect of them falling below the National Minimum Wage.

Health and Safety

The Health and Safety Executive has useful guidance on what health and safety issues might arise from home working.

Home workers provider a unique challenge for employers considering health and safety issues especially due to the lack of control they have over the environment the employee is working in. It is therefore recommended that employers ensure that they have the right to enter the property of home workers in the event they need to take action in respect of risks within the employee's workspace.

A lot of the guidance from the HSE focuses on the mental impact that lone working with minimal supervision can have on employees and puts a key focus on home worker's mental health and how to manage this. The steps that employers should consider taking to protect the mental health of their employees is considered in Chapter 5.

The HSE also makes clear that there are issues that employees and employers need to consider in respect of display equipment. The HSE recommends that an employee who is working from home for any significant period of time should carry out a basic assessment of their workstation and should also be given simple tips on how to reduce risks from display screen work such as taking regular breaks and regularly changing positions. The assessment and tips for employees are again issues which are likely to form part of an employer's home working policy.

CHAPTER SEVEN
HOMEWORKING CONTRACTUAL PROVISIONS AND WHAT TO INCLUDE IN YOUR HOMEWORKING POLICY

Introduction

As detailed in Chapter 4 all employers who may have any employees who may work from home on either a regular basis or an occasional basis should have a home working policy.

Some of the advantages that come from dealing with claims through a home working policy, such as trial periods, are set out in Chapter 4, but in this Chapter we will discuss some of the issues that employers should consider addressing in a home working policy.

As with most policies what works best for employers will depend on their individual circumstances but a degree of flexibility is best as you do not want a policy or contractual provisions which are too inflexible for both parties.

Additionally, home working can result in new clauses or consideration given to what is included in the employee's contract of employment, therefore we will also consider some of the contracted issues that employers may wish to consider.

Place of work

All employees within their contract of employment will need to have specified where their place of work is under s.1 of the ERA. This is no different for home workers.

For those employees who only occasionally work at home it will probably be in the best interests of the employer to keep the employee's place of work as their office address as this gives the employer greater control of the employee.

For those employees who will work either solely or predominantly at home though it is likely that their contract of employment should specify that their place of work is their home address.

Employers should make clear within the contract that the employee may be required to work from other locations and addresses as the employer deems necessary for the performance of their contract of employment. This gives the employer the flexibility to ensure they can require them to work from other locations if necessary but also gives the employee some flexibility to allow them to work from locations such as coffee shops or service stations, subject of course to relevant data protection issues such as these considered in Chapter 11.

The contract should also make sure that a provision is included to make clear that if the employee moves house that they will inform the employee of their new address.

Within any policy an employer should consider specifying the occasions where you might require a home worker to still come into the office such as for team meetings, supervisions or to engage in disciplinary or capability procedures.

Hours of work

Again under s.1 of the ERA an employee's contract of employment should include information about their normal hours of work.

One of the main advantages that home working can offer to employees is the potential for flexibility around their normal working hours. Those working from home can take the opportunity that home working provides to carry out household activities such as taking children to school, taking a dog for a walk or preparing food.

Therefore, the contract of employment should make clear what the expectations are around their hours of work within the contract of employment. There are no set rules around the hours of work for home workers and so employers do not necessarily need to offer employees enhanced flexibility. They could instead require that home workers work the same hours as those employees in an office environment including taking the same breaks, or you could instead have a requirement that home workers carry out a certain amount of work or work a certain amount of hours within a period. This would be a matter to be negotiated between an employer and an employee.

Whatever the situation as detailed in Chapter 6 there can be some real issues in respect of the Working Time Regulations for home workers and you should ensure as an employer you have clauses within the contract to ensure they comply with these issues.

Equipment

One thing that should be considered is whether you will provide necessary equipment to home workers or whether you require them to use their own facilities.

During the Covid-19 outbreak it is likely that due to the sheer number of people working from home and as a result the inevitable unavailability of some equipment that most employers would have relied upon employees using their own equipment such as desks, chairs and in some cases computer equipment. See Chapter 13 for consideration of individuals using their own devices for work purposes.

In normal circumstances there is no requirement for an employer to provide equipment to employees but providing your own equipment can be beneficial partially for data protection purposes e.g. data security as considered in Chapter 10, but also for practical reasons such as ensuring compatibility with employer IT and other systems.

If the employer does provide equipment then consideration should be given to what equipment the employee will be given and other issues such as:

- Can the employee use the equipment for personal reasons;
- If so how much personal use if it may be subject to wear and tear;
- Who is responsible for the maintenance and repair of these items;
- Is the employee liable if the items are damaged:
- Should the items be insured and if so by whom; and
- What happens to these items if the employee leaves the employer's employment.

Clear policies and limits around use of equipment make it easier to configure and justify monitoring arrangements, for more on which see Chapter 15.

Expenses

There is no set rule again about expenses incurred by an employee when they are working from home, it is a matter for negotiation between the parties.

During the COVID -19 outbreak employers will no doubt be aware that there is a government scheme which allows employees to claim £6 per week tax free and they can do this from their employer. However there is no strict requirement for employers to do this and if they choose not to, the employee can instead claim tax relief for that sum from HMRC.

Employers can pay employees expenses above and beyond this £6 per week but there can be tax implications for doing this and so employers should consider if this appropriate in the circumstances. Instead an employer might determine that they are better off reflecting a sum within an employee's salary to account for the expenses an employee might incur especially with difficulties determining sums such as the extra cost an employee might incur in respect of utility bills.

Employers should also consider what impact the employee's place of work might have on mileage expense claims and if for instance an employer pays mileage for attending one of its offices. Whilst it is good practice to pay mileage in these circumstances it is by no means necessary and it is ordinarily a matter of negotiation between the employer and employee.

Right of entry

There are a number of circumstances where an employer may need to access their employee's home if they are home worker. This may be for a health and safety assessment, to repair equipment or to recover equipment following the employee's dismissal.

Therefore, it is good practice to ensure that there is a clause within the employee's contract which allows the employer and its representatives to enter the employee's property for these purposes.

It would be good practice to put some safeguards on this requirement for the benefit of the employee and therefore state that the employer will provide the employee with reasonable notice before exercising this right.

You should also consider the situation if an employee does not have the authority to allow you entry to their residence if they are not the owner or tenant of the property. This for instance might be the case for employees living with their parents. In these circumstances you may wish to ensure that the employee secures permission from the relevant person who can provide the necessary authorities to allow the employer to access the property before agreeing to any home working arrangements.

Issues for the employee to consider

It is worth highlighting in any home working policy things for the employee to consider about their living situation before granting home working to ensure that the employee is not in breach of any legal obligation, these include:

- Ensuring there are no covenants on the property which would prevent the employee from working from home;
- Ensuring that there is nothing in either the employee's mortgage agreement or tenancy agreement which would prevent them from working from home;
- If they are neither the owner of the tenant that they have permission from the owner of the property for the situation;

- Ensuring that working from home would not invalidate their home insurance; and
- Ensuring that there are no planning restrictions which would prevent them from working from home.

The employer should also consider whether they want an employee to check these issues and confirm none are applicable to their circumstances or instead think about what they might do if an employee who has been granted a right to work from home can no longer work from home due to potentially being in breach of one of these legal obligations.

CHAPTER EIGHT
DEALING WITH COMPETING REQUESTS AND BRINGING HOMEWORKING TO AN END

Introduction

It is important that when considering whether an employer should grant home working they also have consideration of the circumstances where they may need to bring home working to an end and how they go about doing this.

The circumstances when an employer may choose to bring a home working arrangement to an end should be relatively rare but there are circumstances where this might happen. It may be that due to changes in the employer's circumstances they can no longer accommodate the employee working from home or there are concerns about the employee continuing to work from home.

The answer to this question is largely dependent on the basis upon which the home working has been agreed, whether it is through a formal flexible working request, agreed in their contract of employment, agreed through a home working policy or is an informal arrangement.

Dealing with competing requests

One difficult an employer might face when considering the possibility for home working is how they approach a situation where the number of requests they have for home working go beyond the number they can accommodate.

The ACAS Code on Flexible Working does deal with this situation when a request is made via the statutory flexible working process and provides the following guidance:

- An employer is not required to make a determination on which request is feels has the most merit and should look at the request in the context of its business.
- Requests should be dealt with in the order in which they were received and employers should, when considering later requests, assess the impact on the business in light of the existing home working arrangements
- Employers should consider having a discussion with the employees who have made the request to see if there are any compromises that can be made to try and accommodate all the requests.

Despite the recommendations from the ACAS Code on Flexible Working there are some circumstances where it would be appropriate to consider the reasoning behind the employee making the request and this should take precedence over considering the time frames in which requests were received.

Preference would ordinarily be given to those who had a reason under the Equality Act to request the change, with an employee with a disability likely to be given priority if home working may be a reasonable adjustment. Employers should be careful though if they choose to prioritise a request on sex discrimination and care grounds as this could arguably result in a sex discrimination claim from a male employee.

The ACAS Code on Flexible Working would only apply to statutory flexible working requests but it does seem sensible to use the guidance when considering requests through other circumstances as well.

How the request is made could also factor into an employer's decision-making process. If a request is made through the home working policy but one employee meets the eligibility criteria for a statutory flexible working request and another does not then it would seem to be reasonable to prioritise the employee who is eligible under the statutory flexible working scheme over the other employee.

In the vast majority of circumstances it is unlikely that it would be reasonable to remove an existing home working arrangement from an employee no matter the circumstances of the person making the later request. An employer may wish to speak to their existing home workers to see if any were willing to change their situation to accommodate another employee's request to show they had done everything reasonable in considering the request but removing the home working situation of an existing home worker is in all likelihood unreasonable.

Ending an agreement reached through a statutory flexible working request or a contractual arrangement

The process for ending a home working scheme agreed through the statutory flexible working scheme and a contractual arrangement are similar as the effect of the statutory flexible working scheme is that it creates a permanent change to the employee's terms and conditions and as such it should be treated as if the employee has a contractual right to work from home.

Therefore, in both circumstances you would need to treat a change to the home working arrangements of an employee as you would any normal contractual change. Often a requirement for an employee to no longer work from home can result from the employee securing a promotion where their new role doesn't suit home working. In that situation it should hopefully have been made clear to the employee before the promotion and so the removal of home working should be relatively uncontroversial.

If the removal of home working is for other reasons then the employer would need to consult with the employee about the change and the proposed reasoning behind it and ultimately if you couldn't reach agreement on the change the employer would need to consider dismissing the employee and then re-engaging them.

In terms of the reasoning behind ending an employee's home working there is nothing within the statutory flexible working request regime that deals with bringing a formally agreed flexible working scheme to an end. However it would appear prudent that if an employer is seeking to end a flexible working arrangement its reason for doing so is one of the reasons that an employer can reject a request for as set out in s.80G of the ERA which is covered in Chapter 3.

One thing for the employer to consider is what if they can no longer accommodate home working for an employee who primarily or solely works from home. In these circumstances an employer will need to determine if they would have a role for the employee at their office and if they did whether it would be reasonable for the employee to have to travel to the office.

If these options are not available then it is likely that the only alternative option would be dismissal, which may be either by reason of redundancy or some other substantial reason depending on the circumstances. As this decision may result in a potential claim for unfair dismissal, employers should be confident they have a good business reason for the removal of home working and have properly consulted with the employee to consider alternatives to dismissal.

Ending an agreement through a home working policy

As set out in Chapter 4, if an employee agrees a home working situation through a home working policy then a well drafted policy will have provisions in place allowing the employer a high degree of flexibility when considering if it is necessary to bring the home working arrangement to an end.

Despite any flexibility in the policy if the home working has existed for long enough then it may be that there is a contractual right due to custom and practice. Therefore even when an employer is relying upon terms within its home working policy to bring a practice to an end it should consider if it has existed for a sufficiently long period that the right to work from home now forms part of the employee's contract of employment.

Ending an "informal arrangement"

A common issue which can occur with any informal arrangement, is whether if that arrangement has existed for some time it can be said to form part of the contract through custom and practice.

The implication of term through of custom and practice within employment contracts is a very detailed area but in basic terms for a term to be implied via custom and practice it must be "*reasonable, notorious and certain*" and followed "*because there is a sense of legal obligation to do so*". In practice this means in the context of home working that if an employer allowed employees to work from home in certain occasions and had always allowed this there may be an argument that there was an implied term allowing home working in those circumstances.

In addition to custom and practice an employee may also argue that where an agreement had been made with their employer in respect of a home working arrangement, albeit in an informal manner, that this might be sufficient to suggest there had been an agreement to vary the employee's terms of employment.

This situation was considered by the Employment Appeal Tribunal in the case *Ms Grace France v Westminster City Council* [1]. In this case Ms France's role required her to regularly attend conferences and her manager had agreed with her than when attending conferences she could work from home and go straight to the conference from home or return home from the conference and work upon her return. The manager agreed to this as a matter of administrative convenience. Her employer then subsequently ended this practice due to concerns of having confidential information at the employee's home address and Ms France resigned and claimed constructive dismissal. The Employment Appeal Tribunal agreed that she had not been constructively dismissed and put considerable weight on the fact that the employer had a home working policy but the agreement had not been reached through this process.

This case shows the value of having a home working policy in place as in these circumstances it might have been that this informal practice may have been found to have been a contractual term had it not been for the fact it had not been agreed through the existing formal process.

Risks of removing an employee's right to home working

The risks of ending an employee's right to work from home are very similar to those set out in Chapter 4, if a request through a home working policy is rejected.

The one key issue to consider is that there is a greater risk attached to removing a home working requirement than not granting one and it is more likely to result in a constructive dismissal claim for an employer if they choose to do this. An employer therefore needs to be confident in the business case it has and its justification why it needs to remove the home working requirement in case it is challenged.

---

1 *EAT/0214/02*

CHAPTER NINE
HOMEWORKING AND DATA PROTECTION

This element of the book sets out the data protection considerations and implications for home working. In May 2018, the data protection regime in the UK was overhauled by the General Data Protection Regulation (EU) 2016/679 ('the GDPR') which was directly implemented into UK law. Sitting alongside the GDPR, is the Data Protection Act 2018 ('DPA 2018') which supplements the requirements set out in the GDPR and sets out UK-specific exemptions to the GDPR as well as making the UK version of the GDPR into UK legislation. Therefore, the two main pieces of data protection legislation which organisations must consider are the GDPR and the DPA 2018.

The GDPR applies to a vast variety of organisations, across multiple sectors and throughout the whole of the European Union – it cannot provide specific requirements and does not include any specific examples in relation to home working. What it does is provide a set of data protection principles and rules and leaves the interpretation to individual organisations.

In this section, we aim to consider the data protection principles, apply them to the concept of home working and provide you with practical guidance to assist you with complying with data protection law.

Data Protection Principles

The GDPR sets out several key data protection principles which organisations must comply with when processing personal data[1]. These data protection principles state that personal data must be:

1 Article 5 General Data Protection Regulation (EU) 2016/679

- Processed lawfully, fairly and in a transparent manner (**'the lawfulness, fairness and transparency principle'**);

- Collected for specified, explicit and legitimate purposes and not further processed in a manner that is incompatible with those purposes (**'the purpose limitation principle'**);

- Adequate, relevant and limited to what is necessary in relation to the purposes for which they are processed (**'the data minimisation principle'**);

- Accurate and, where necessary, up to date; every necessary step must be taken to ensure that inaccurate personal data is erased or rectified without delay (**'the accuracy principle'**);

- Kept in a form which permits identification of data subjects for no longer than is necessary for the purposes of which the personal data is processed (**'the storage limitation principle'**);

- Processed in a manner that ensures appropriate security of the personal data, including protection against unauthorised or unlawful processing and against accidental loss, destruction or damage, using appropriate technical or organisational measures (**'the integrity and confidentiality principle'**); and

- Finally, organisations must also be responsible for, and able to demonstrate, compliance with all of these principles (**'the accountability principle'**).

The Role of the Information Commissioner's Office

The Information Commissioner's Office (ICO) is the UK's independent body set up to uphold information rights (including rights under data protection legislation, freedom of information legislation and environmental information regulations).

In terms of data protection, the ICO is responsible for:

- Ensuring organisations use and process personal information in accordance with the law;
- Maintaining a register of Controllers;
- Handling concerns or complaints from members of the public and organisations about the use of personal information; and
- Conducting investigations and prosecutions into organisations and individuals that misuse personal information.

The ICO has a number of investigative and enforcement powers it can take against an organisation or an individual for breaching data protection laws. It can:

- Record the fact that there has been a breach of data protection law but take no further action;
- Investigate circumstances surrounding a breach of data protection law and any remedial action that has already been taken;
- Require a Controller to undertake a course of action to prevent further breaches of data protection law;
- Take formal enforcement action turning such a requirement into a legal obligation;
- Conduct onsite asssessments including entering premises, accessing documents and interviewing specified persons; and
- Where there is a serious breach of the GDPR, the ICO may serve a monetary penalty notice up to the value of €20 million or 4% of annual global turnover, whichever is higher.

In addition to the formal enforcement powers set out above, action that is taken by the ICO is published on its website and commonly picked up by the media so can have an effect on an organisation's reputation. In addition to action being taken by the ICO, affected individuals now have the opportunity to claim for compensation for distress caused by a personal data breach.

Therefore, complying with data protection is important from a financial, regulatory and reputational point of view as the ramifications of breaches of data protection law can have a long-lasting impact on organisations.

CHAPTER TEN
DATA SECURITY IN THE HOME ENVIRONMENT

<u>The Law</u>

For the purposes of this section of the book, we will be concentrating on the 'integrity and confidentiality principle' of the GDPR and looking at the practical measures organisations should take to demonstrate compliance with the GDPR.

The integrity and confidentiality principle of the GDPR states that organisations must process personal data in a manner that ensures appropriate security of the personal information, including protection against unauthorised or unlawful processing and against accidental loss, destruction or damage, using appropriate technical or organisational measures[1].

The integrity and confidentiality principle is supplemented by Article 32 of the GDPR which sets out some more detailed security measures that must be in place to protect personal information. However, it is not prescriptive. Article 32 of the GDPR adopts a risk-based approach to allow organisations to ensure a level of security appropriate to the level of risk your data processing poses. In assessing the risk of a breach of security, organisations should consider:

- The state of the art and the costs of implementation;
- The nature, scope, context and purposes of the processing as well as the risk of varying likelihood and severity for the rights and freedoms of individuals; and

1 Article 5(1)(f) General Data Protection Regulation (EU) 2016/679

- The risks that are presented by your data processing in particular from accidental or unlawful destruction, loss, alteration, unauthorised disclosure of, or access to personal information.

Taking into account these considerations, Article 32 suggests the following ways to ensure an appropriate level of risk:

- Pseudonymisation and encryption of personal information;
- The ability to ensure the ongoing confidentiality, integrity, availability and resilience of processing systems and services;
- The ability to restore the availability and access to personal information in a timely manner in the event of a physical or technical incident; and
- A process for regularly testing, assessing and evaluating the effectiveness of technical and organisational measures for ensuring the security of the processing.

Applying the Law to Home working

Home working poses a number of implications for the integrity and confidentiality principle which organisations must consider. Even though many organisations regard home working as a positive development, it also presents an area of additional risk for an organisation. Whilst working at home, staff that have remote access to your network and systems are not bound by the physical security measures that may be in place at your office premises to prevent unauthorised access to your systems. The usual technical and organisational measures that you had in place to protect personal information in the office environment may no longer be appropriate if the majority of your workforce are working from home. Without the implementation of appropriate technical measures to address the risks posed by home working, the risk of unauthorised access to your systems increases and may result in the loss or destruction of personal information, including personal information of staff or customers or clients, which you may hold.

The ICO recognised during the Covid-19 pandemic that there has been unprecedented demand for home working and confirmed that data protection law does not prohibit or hinder home working. However, you should take time to ensure the solutions you put in place for home working are secure.

Below we have set out a number of areas organisations must consider when deciding to implement a home working policy. These elements should all be considered within a Data Protection Impact Assessment (DPIA) in order to assess the risks posed by home working and the measures that are put in place to reduce these risks. For further details, please see ***'The Importance of DPIAs'*** below.

Importance of Policies and Procedures

The security requirements in the GDPR go beyond the technical measures, they also include organisational measures that are put in place to ensure the security of personal information. One key organisational measure in relation to home working is the implementation of appropriate security policies for homeworkers.

You should have policy documents in place for staff who work from home which confirm how personal information should be handled, accessed and disposed of. It should be clear to staff that the same data protection considerations apply equally in the home environment as they do in the office.

Remote Access

Permitting staff to access your systems remotely enables staff to work effectively from home as they have access to the same information as they would have when working in the office. The particular IT solution you choose to enable your staff to access your systems remotely is outside the scope of this book, but we have set out some considerations to take into account when making that choice or reviewing the remote access solution that you already have in place.

Whether access to work information should be restricted via a specific app or the use of encrypted email protocols should be considered by organisations as accessing the organisation's network via an unsecure "coffee house" network could increase the risk of information being lost. Therefore, use of a secure virtual private network (VPN) when not in an office environment should be a fundamental requirement. The ICO recommends the use of a multi-factor authentication to access systems and networks remotely so that it is more difficult for your system to be accessed by an unauthorised user in the event a user's log-in details are compromised[2]. Similarly, staff should be reminded on a regular basis to use complex and unique passwords and this requirement should be included within your security policies.

Confidential Waste

As part of your planning for home working, you must consider how confidential waste is to be disposed of outside the office environment. This may include requiring staff to ensure confidential waste is disposed of securely themselves, providing shredders or arranging for confidential waste to be collected by the organisation and then disposed of securely. The measures that you implement will largely depend on the level of risk faced by your particular organisation. Alternatively, you may decide

2 https://ico.org.uk/for-organisations/working-from-home/working-from-home-security-checklists-for-employers/

to require homeworkers to be paperless which would therefore reduce the risk of paperwork being lost or disposed of incorrectly. There are also technical measures which can be put in place to reduce the amount of paperwork being produced, for example prohibiting printers from being connected to your organistion's equipment or network. If it is necessary to grant some workers access to printers, authorised users could be permitted to connect a printer provided that they are informed of the need to dispose of the waste securely.

Any measures you put in place to address the risks posed by confidential waste should be documented within your data protection policies and procedures and any data protection impact assessment you decide to conduct. For further details, please see ***'The Importance of Data Protection Impact Assessments'*** below.

Use of Apps

During the Covid-19 crisis many organisations looked at innovative ways to keep in touch with colleagues, clients and customers. This has inevitably involved the use of new technology and, given the urgent timescales involved, the use of this new technology has probably not received the usual level of scrutiny before its use has been permitted by an organisation.

Staff should be reminded that they should only use apps and technology approved by your organisation for work purposes. When approving a particular app or technology for use by your organisation, you will be required to assess the level of security the platform has in place and how it will comply with the GDPR. You will also need to ensure staff correctly implement the security features provided by the platform as these may not always be installed automatically.

The use of apps and technology should be set out clearly within your home working policies and procedures and confirm that only approved apps and technology should be used for work purposes. It may also be necessary to consider the use of any apps or technology in any data protection impact assessment you decide to conduct. For further details, see *'The Importance of Data Protection Impact Assessments'* below.

Data Breach Procedure

One of the main changes introduced by the GDPR was the requirement for personal data breaches to be reported to the ICO within 72 hours in certain circumstances[3]. There is also a duty to communicate the breach to individuals in certain circumstances.

The obligation to report personal data breaches is set out in Article 33 of the GDPR:

> *"In the case of a personal data breach, the controller shall without undue delay and, where feasible, no later than 72 hours after having become aware of it, notify the personal data breach to the Supervisory Authority... unless the personal data breach is unlikely to result in a risk to the rights freedoms of natural persons".*

The 72-hour reporting timescale begins from the time the organisation becomes aware of the breach, which may not necessarily be 72 hours from the time in which the correct person within your organisation is made aware of the breach. Given the very short period of time involved, your organisation should have a data breach procedure in place where staff escalate suspected breaches promptly so that an assessment can be made regarding whether the breach should be reported to the ICO.

It is important that staff are made aware of the need to continue to report breaches whilst working from home. Your data breach procedure should allow for staff to report breaches remotely and include provision for who to contact in relation to a breach out of normal office hours.

3 Article 33 General Data Protection Regulation (EU) 2016/679

Regular reminders should also be sent to staff about the continued need to report suspected data breaches in accordance with your data breach procedure.

It is likely that as we get used to a new way of working, you may see an increase in the number of data breaches being reported, for example e-mails being sent to the wrong email address or account log-in details being compromised. Your data breach procedure should include provision to take into account a 'lessons learned' exercise following any actual or suspected personal data breach. As part of your investigation into the personal data breach, you should be able to determine whether the breach was a result of human error or it was a more systematic issue and highlight what action can be taken to prevent the breach from occurring. This may include:

- Considering whether or not any of your policies and procedures need updating or amending;
- Considering whether any training needs have been identified; and
- Considering how effective your data breach procedure was – does it need reviewing or is any further training required?

Your lessons learned review following a personal data breach should be carefully documented and any changes required implemented in a timely manner in an attempt to avoid a recurrence, particularly whilst we get used to this new way of working.

Summary

To summarise, prior to implementing home working or reviewing your existing home working policies and procedures, you should take the following steps in order to demonstrate compliance with data protection law:

1. What technological security measures do we need to put in place to keep information secure in the home environment?

2. What security measures do we need to put in place to handle confidential waste?

3. Have you completed a Data Protection Impact Assessment to assess the risks to individuals and identify the measures you need to put in place to mitigate those risks?

4. Do you need to update your data protection compliance documents such as privacy notices, data protection policies and records of processing activities?

5. Do your staff need any additional training on data breaches, data protection and home working?

To assist you in considering each of these points, a data protection security checklist has been included at Appendix A of this book.

CHAPTER ELEVEN
ACCESS AND IDENTITY

In this section:

- Why do access and identity go together?
- How does Data Protection apply to access and identity?
- How does home and agile working make a difference to access and identity?
- What are the risks in relation to access and identity?
- How should organisations address those risks?

Why Do Access and Identity Go Together?

Access to where data are held (including buildings and IT systems) is usually subject to some controls. Those controls are commonly based on verifying the identity of the person requesting access and the degree of access that person is permitted.

Application of the data security principle includes controlling access to data and ideally operating a system that is capable of allowing different levels of access to different types and volumes of data. That makes identifying users and their respective degrees of permitted access critically important.

How Does Data Protection Apply to Access and Identity?

Data Protection comes into play in two ways which can overlap.

The first is that identity will involve using an individual's personal data in one way or another, for example their image on a security pass or their username and password in an IT system. The way in which the organisation uses these personal data and how it protects them from loss or misuse will be governed by GDPR and the Data Protection Act. In this way the day subject is the person whose identity information is being handled by the organisation.

The second way is that the use of identity data to control access to other people's personal data is covered by the data security principle and the data security duty imposed on data controllers and data processors in the GDPR. In this way the identity is a security measure used to protect the third-party personal data.

Access and identity is a prime example of the GDPR's requirement for "technical and organisational measures" in the field of data security. Using identity as a way to control access requires both technical and organisational elements to be aligned and effective. A technically sound working method can be undermined by deficient policies and management of how it is used.

Organisations should avoid falling into the trap of establishing a technically effective method and then assuming that their individual users will both understand and respect it sufficiently to maintain its effectiveness without any guidance or management. Poor implementation can ruin a plan which would be effective if done properly.

How does home and agile working make a difference to access and identity?

Applying access and identity solutions where individuals have moved to home or agile working requires a review of risk assessments, data mapping and the record of processing to establish what is different and what changes are needed.

Access controls in an office setting are simpler because the organisation can control perimeter access to its building and within that can apply system and storage access controls with ongoing supervision by managers in the same location as the individual users. All of that changes with majority or total home or agile working.

Access to a home setting and especially a public space such as a café or hotel is not controlled by the organisation and as lockdown restrictions are relaxed that becomes an increasing issue. Even where access to a home is limited to family members devices may be viewed and shared in a way that would not happen in an office setting. Children very rarely come into an office setting to use the organisation's IT resources to do their schoolwork. With home schooling as widespread as home working that might not be the case. Shared devices or devices connected to the same private user account (e.g. Apple ID or Amazon) will share information and sometimes display alerts on all devices at once. For more on this please see the sections on use of personal devices for work purposes and data security generally.

The outer layer of organisational security having been removed by home or agile working there is a lot more reliance on the second element of identity-based access to data and IT systems. If users are having to do more remote log-ins with unfamiliar new system requirements or appearances they are more vulnerable to phishing attacks. The organisation as the data controller for their system profiles is responsible for taking steps to maintain security of those data.

What are the risks in relation to identity and access?

In assessing the risks it is important to remember both aspects of personal data that are in play: the home worker's login credentials as their personal data and the personal data contained in the systems accessed using the home worker's login credentials.

The risk relating to the home worker's login credentials is that if they are subject to a confidentiality breach and accessed by a third party they could be used in identity theft and/or attacks on other accounts held by that individual. This is the risk created when account access details for online user accounts are compromised as has happened recently in relation to for example loyalty card accounts. Criminals obtaining those details would then try the same username and password to gain access to other accounts including online banking.

If there is more reliance on remote system access that might mean more instances of forgotten passwords or lock-outs through failed login attempts (including those caused by keyboard cleaning if the machine is not turned off) and so more access to login credentials may be needed to support users. Where and how those are stored as a data set is critical as well is access control. User support with logins is essential and it may not be an option not to keep a record of users' login credentials.

An availability breach relating to the login credentials would prevent user support and so access to the system. This would be a failsafe situation to some degree as the result would be no access and the remedy a reset of user details. The risk here may lie in the delay it would cause in users being able to access systems and do their jobs.

The risks in relation to third party personal data ordinarily protected by the login credentials are far-reaching. If hackers obtain login credentials they can gain access to the organisation's systems without being detected because the system will recognise a legitimate login unless there is dual factor authentication in place (for more on which see below). With system access hackers can obtain more personal information from address books and contacts, view and copy documents including personal data, infect the system with malware and send further malicious emails which will appear to come from the organisation because they do. Once details of other individuals taken from the system are in the hands of hackers they will use and/or sell on the information for use in attacking accounts of those other people with the aim of getting into bank or retail accounts with payment details. Internal information of the organisation can be used in "spear phishing" attacks in which emails appear to be genuine internal payment requests or requests for further information.

How Should Organisations Address Those Risks?

There are a number of options available to organisations to address these risks in both parts of the analysis. The GDPR and Data Protection Act require "appropriate technical and organisational measures" to protect personal data against "unauthorised or unlawful processing and against accidental loss, destruction or damage"[1].

User Login Credentials

Both technical and organisational measures are relevant here. Technical measures would include the security applied to where login information is held in the IT system to make it harder for anyone with unauthorised system access to obtain login details for other users and potentially some secondary password requirement for users requesting a password reset.

Organisational measures would include the policies that apply to system use, passwords and other login credentials and ensuring awareness of how serious a matter it is to share or disclose login information. If it can be demonstrated through an investigation that an individual caused a data breach through not looking after login credentials properly that

1 GDPR Article 5(1)(f) "integrity and confidentiality"

may be a basis for disciplinary action in the same way as it would be if an individual did not take care of keys or alarm codes for a physical office and in effect left the door open.

System Access Using User Login Credentials

One technical next step on top of having a password is to implement dual-factor authentication for remote access to the organisation's systems. This requires the correct password for the user and then a further code which is generated for each login and so will not be valid for another login. Dual-factor authentication codes can be generated by separate devices (as offered by some banks) or by an application installed on a mobile phone.

That creates the secondary question of the access security of the device on which the dual-factor authentication application is installed and the safe storage of any separate device. That may be addressed by a combination of technical actions such as device access controls on mobile phones and organisational measures such as polices about how to maintain IT security in a home working environment[2].

Data loss protection (DLP) software is increasingly used by organisations as a way to detect unauthorised activity in IT systems and prevent or minimise data security breaches. Different options have different features and in general DLP systems operate by looking for what are defined by the administrators of the system as unusual or suspicious patterns of system access and use as well as sweeping the contents and destinations of emails for suspicious or anomalous content or recipients. The use of algorithms to identify patterns or anomalies sometimes results in these systems being marketed as "artificial intelligence" and some systems require an upload of historic email traffic for users in order to establish a picture of what is identified as normal for their use of email.

---

2 See Chapter 7 (Home Working Contractual Provisions and What to Include in Your Home Working Policy), Chapter 9 (Home Working and Data Protection) and Chapter 10 (Data Security in the Home Environment)

DLP systems are specifically identified in the EPBD Opinion on workplace monitoring as an example of technology that could be invasive systemic monitoring requiring a high degree of benefit to balance the degree of intrusion into what may be private use of the email system. One recommendation is to reduce the degree of oversight by configuring the system to generate warnings to users before email is sent giving the opportunity to undo any mistakes before they cause a problem or to post a justification for apparently problematic communications. Email and attachment checking can be configured to look for high volumes of personal identifiable information or strings of numbers that resemble bank account numbers or telephone numbers with a view to catching inappropriate disclosures of personal data before they happen. DLP systems can also monitor transfers of data within the system such as files being copied from one location to another and especially to removable storage devices[3].

Use of this kind of technology requires an DPIA before implementation[4]. That should involve setting the objectives of using the software and considering how its use should be supported and controlled using appropriate polices and procedures. There is a risk of “click fatigue” if users have to work through excessive volumes of warnings. Having too many warnings increases the chance that users will click to dismiss them instead of pausing to read them and react to them. That could result in the kind of emails being sent that the system is there to prevent. Enforcing a policy, justifying the degree of monitoring and establishing the security measures as appropriate in the event of a breach will all be assisted by calibrating any DLP system carefully.

3 For more on monitoring see Chapter 14

4 For more on DPIAs see Chapter 17

CHAPTER TWELVE
USE OF PERSONAL DEVICES FOR WORK PURPOSES

Remote working is not new, but recent events mean that there is now a signification proportion of workforces working remotely. Given the large numbers of remote workers, many organisations are permitting staff to work remotely on their own personal devices (commonly known as 'Bring Your Own Device' or BYOD).

Whilst there are significant costs saving in permitting staff to work remotely on their own devices, organisations (the controller) will have less control over the device than if it was owned by the organisation. This can raise a number of risks from a data protection perspective as the device will be owned and controlled by a member of staff rather than the employer.

The Law

For the purposes of this section of the book, we will be concentrating on the 'integrity and confidentiality principle' of the GDPR and looking at the practical measures organisations should take to demonstrate compliance with the GDPR when adopting a BYOD policy.

The integrity and confidentiality principle of the GDPR states that organisations must process personal data in a manner that ensures appropriate security of the personal information, including protection against unauthorised or unlawful processing and against accidental loss, destruction or damage, using appropriate technical or organisational measures[1]. Therefore, organisations must have appropriate security measures

1 Article 5(1)(f) General Data Protection Regulation (EU) 2016/679

in place to prevent the personal information the organisation holds from being lost, stolen or used inappropriately.

This can pose a challenge where an organisation's information is being accessed, stored and used on a personal device. In order to comply with the integrity and confidentiality principle of the GDPR, organisations must remain in control of its personal information regardless of who owns the device the work is carried out on[2].

BYOD Risks

Before adopting a BYOD policy or permitting the use of BYOD, organisations should be aware of the risks posed by BYOD in order that technical and organisational security measures can be put into place to mitigate the effect of these risks. Some of the data protection risks of BYOD include:

- Loss or theft of the device;
- Unauthorised access to the device;
- Loss of control of organisation information (e.g. the organisation being unaware the information exists as it is not stored within its own network or system);
- Information being used inappropriately and/or a blurring of the lines between personal and business use;
- Vulnerabilities or malicious software being introduced to an organisation's systems via a personal device;
- Lack of security software on the personal device; and

2 ICO Bring Your Own Device Guidance

- Business information being retained at the end of the employment relationship.

In order to address each of these issues, a data protection impact assessment should be carried out and a BYOD policy should be implemented so that staff know the risks of connecting their devices to your systems and are aware of their responsibilities.

Data Protection Impact Assessment

Before permitting the use of BYOD or implementing a BYOD policy you should consider conducting a data protection impact assessment (DPIA).

The GDPR introduced an obligation on controllers to conduct a DPIA where processing presents a high risk to individuals' interests[3]. The use of DPIAs is a key element of ensuring privacy by design and by default and demonstrating accountability for GDPR compliance. In most cases it is likely that a DPIA should be carried prior to permitting BYOD or implementing a BYOD policy.

Even if you do not consider the use of BYOD to present a high risk to the individuals' interests, DPIAs are examples of best practice when implementing new technology and will demonstrate compliance with the GDPR. A DPIA will also address at outset any issues you may face further down the line (e.g. how do we stop staff saving information on their own device? How will we protect our information if the device is lost?) and therefore can save you time in long run.

A DPIA is a process to assess and minimise the data protection risks of a project. It may not be possible to ensure that there is no risk at all to individuals but conducting a DPIA will assist you in minimising the risk to individuals and assessing whether or not the level of risk is acceptable

3 Article 35 General Data Protection Regulation (EU) 2016/679

in the circumstances, taking into account the benefits of the technology you want to implement.

There is no standard template to use when conducting a DPIA. The GDPR states that a DPIA that contains at least[4]:

- A systematic description of the envisaged processing operations and the purposes of the processing, including, where applicable, the legitimate interest pursued by the controller;
- An assessment of the necessity and proportionality of the processing operations in relation to the purposes;
- An assessment of the risks to the rights and freedoms of individuals;
- The measures envisaged to address the risks, including safeguards, security measures and mechanisms to ensure the protection of personal data and to demonstrate compliance with the GDPR taking into account the rights and legitimate interests of individuals.

A template DPIA can be found at Appendix B. However, we have set out below some of the considerations you should take into account when conducting your DPIA and drafting a BYOD policy.

<u>Suitability of the device</u>

You will need to consider the suitability of a member of staff's device before permitting them to access your systems and network. Not only should the device be able to cope with the practical demands of the work required but the security capacities of the device should meet your organisation's minimum standard. Staff should be required to confirm

---

4 Article 35(7) General Data Protection Regulation (EU) 2016/679

that their device's operating system is up to data and that relevant patches have been downloaded. Additionally, staff should be warned of the risks of downloading unverified apps to their device as these may increase the risk of malicious software being introduced to the organisation's network.

Storing Personal Information

When considering implementing YOD, you will need to consider where your organisation's personal information will be stored. This may include:

- On the staff's own personal device;
- On the organisation's network;
- In a cloud.

Wherever the personal data is being stored, you will need to consider how to keep that information safe and secure and unable to be accessed by unauthorised third parties. The 'integrity and confidentiality' principle is much easier to satisfy if the personal information is being stored on the organisation's network or within a private cloud account. If personal information is being stored on the actual device, the risk of it being accessed by unauthorised users (e.g. other family members) is much greater. Also, if the device is lost or stolen it is unlikely to be encrypted in the same way as a work issued device and risks personal information being accessed and used inappropriately.

There are technological solutions available which enable work information to be segregated from staff's personal use of their device. This prevents company information being stored on the actual device and information can be kept within your control. The ICO recommends using multi-factor authentication to access an organisation's network and systems remotely to avoid unauthorised third parties accessing your network in the event a member of staff's log in credentials are compromised[5].

From a practical perspective, where copies of information (such as PDFs and word documents) are stored on many different devices, there is an increased risk that the information will become out-of-date or inaccurate over time. There is also a risk that information will be retained for longer than is necessary, and organisations may face difficulties keeping track of copies. Organisations might therefore find it problematic responding on time to a subject access requests, as having to search multiple devices, some of which the organisation might not be aware of, will only slow the process. Prohibiting work information from being stored on or saved to a personal device will also help ensure you are able to comply requests to exercise data protection rights (e.g. a subject access request). If information is not stored within an organisation's system, then it is difficult to search for that information in the event a subject access request is received. For further information, please see ***'Home working and Subject Access Requests'*** below.

Finally, organisations must also consider how it deals with staff who engage with BYOD when leaving their employment. Provision to retrieve stored documents and delete relevant information from the device should be incorporated into your BYOD policy.

Loss or Theft of a Personal Device

Prior to permitting BYOD or implementing a BYOD policy, you must consider what would happen in the event the personal device is lost or stolen and what organisational information could be obtained if the device fell into the wrong hands. A device's geo-locations should be switched on and a capability to remotely wipe data if the device is lost

5 https://ico.org.uk/for-organisations/working-from-home/bring-your-own-device-what-should-we-consider/

or stolen should be a prerequisite to using a personal device for work purposes.

The need to be able to remotely wipe the organisation's information also supports the segregation of work and personal aspects of the device. If the elements can be segregated, then there is the ability to remotely wipe only the segregated work information rather than the entire contents of the device.

Any device tracking capability should only be used for the purposes of locating the device in the event it is lost or stolen. It should not be used to track or monitor staff. Staff who use their personal devices for work purposes should made aware of how their device will be tracked. This may be included be included within your staff privacy notices and your BYOD policy. For further information in relation to monitoring your staff, please see Monitoring home and agile working.

Staff must also be aware that the loss or theft of a personal device subject to BYOD may be a personal data breach. Therefore, staff must report any actual or suspected loss or theft of their device in accordance with your data breach procedure so that measures can be taken to reduce the risk of the information on the device being accessed (e.g. by remotely wiping the device). Thought should be given to how staff can make such reports whilst they are out of the office and must be aware that your usual IT security, acceptable use and data protection policies all apply as much to a device subject to BYOD as they do to your office IT equipment.

Purpose Limitation

The use of personal devices for work purposes might also raise the risk that personal information is processed for different purposes from which it was originally collected. To counter this risk, you need to ensure your staff are aware of their responsibilities in terms of only using work information for work purposes. Staff should be reminded that the use of their personal devices for work purposes is subject to all your organisation's usual policies and procedures. Training may need to be provided in this regard prior to implementing BYOD or permitting staff to use personal devices for work purposes.

Assessment of Risks

As discussed above, you should conduct a DPIA prior to permitting BYOD or implementing a BYOD policy. The requirements for a conducting a DPIA are set out in more detail in '***The Importance of Data Protection Impact Assessments***' above. However, we have set out below some of the specific considerations to incorporate into your BYOD DPIA.

Taking the elements of a DPIA required by the GDPR and applying them to the use of BYOD, we suggest reviewing the following considerations:

- **Description of the processing and the purpose of the processing** – This should be a general description of the use of personal devices for work purposes and your reasons for implementing this technology including the benefits from cost savings, increased confidence in staff using equipment they are familiar with and the business need for staff to work from home in response to the Covid-19 pandemic;

- **An assessment of the necessity and proportionality of BYOD** – In order to assess the necessity and proportionality of the use of BYOD, you should include details of how you will ensure data protection compliance as this is a good measure of necessity and proportionality. Guidance from the Article 29 Data Protection Working Party (now known as the European Data Protection

Board) states that when assessing necessity and proportionality, you should include details of the following[6]:

- Your lawful basis for processing;
- How you will comply with the 'purpose limitation' principle (e.g. how you will prevent a blurring of the lines of personal and business information and prevent business information being used for staff's own purposes);
- How you will comply with the 'data minimisation' principle (e.g. how you will avoid multiple copies of information being stored in different areas and on different devices);
- How you will provide privacy information to individuals (e.g. by updating your privacy notices and data protection policies);
- How you will keep information subject to BYOD secure (e.g. the technical IT solution you adopt to use BYOD); and
- How you will comply with individual rights' requests (e.g. by ensuring business information is not saved on personal devices);

- **An assessment of the risks to the rights and freedoms of individuals** – In order to assess the risks that BYOD poses to the rights and freedoms of individuals, it is important to be clear that risk is not limited to fraud or financial loss. It can also include the inability to exercise data protection rights, the loss of control over their personal information, loss of confidentiality,

6 WP29 Guidelines on Data Protection Impact Assessment and determining whether processing is "likely to result in high risk" for the purposes of Regulation 2016/679 (WP248)

reputational damage and identity theft or fraud[7]. As part of this assessment, you should consider what risk there will be to individuals in the event of a data security breach including unauthorised access to meetings. Common risks posed by BYOD include:

- unauthorised third parties gaining access to work information held on personal devices;
- loss or theft of personal devices;
- inappropriate use of work information for their own personal use by staff;
- staff not implementing the appropriate security settings on their device; and
- staff storing and saving work information on their own device.

- **Measures in place to mitigate the risks that you have identified** – Once you have identified the risks posed by BYOD, you should then identify what measures you can put in place to mitigate against each of the risks identified. This may include:
  - Deciding that certain devices are unsuitable to be used for work purposes as they lack the appropriate security settings;
  - Taking additional technical security measures;
  - Providing additional training to staff to ensure they know how to apply the correct security settings to their devices;
  - Preparing internal guidance or protocols;

7 https://ico.org.uk/for-organisations/guide-to-data-protection/guide-to-the-general-data-protection-regulation-gdpr/data-protection-impact-assessments-dpias/

- Amending your privacy notices, record of processing activity and data protection policies to include reference to BYOD;
- Ensuring staff are aware that the organisation's usual data protection policies and procedures apply equally to their use of their own device for work purposes.

Once your DPIA has been completed, the measures you propose to mitigate against the identified risks should be implemented and recorded on the DPIA. The DPIA should then be kept under review, particularly where the use of technology is involved, as practices and technology will change rapidly over time and technical security measures are likely to become outdated quickly.

CHAPTER THIRTEEN
VIDEO CONFERENCING

Video conferencing has been a useful tool for organisations to keep in touch and stay connected with their staff, customers, clients, suppliers and prospects throughout the Covid-19 crisis. Many of the most common video conferencing platforms were unheard of prior to the crisis but are now household names.

Due to the urgent need to get staff set up for home working quickly, it is no surprise that some video conferencing tools have been implemented without the usual level of scrutiny as to their security and suitability. As the dust is settling and we get used to the 'new normal', consideration should be given to your choice of video conferencing provider to determine whether it is the best tool for the job.

Security Requirements

An important point to consider when appointing a video conferencing provider, is to assess the level of security the provider has in place and how it will comply with the GDPR. A video conferencing provider will, in most cases, be a Data Processor and the organisation using the video conferencing technology will be a Controller for the purposes of the GDPR. Therefore your organisation, as the Controller, must only appoint a Data Processor that can provide sufficient guarantees to implement appropriate technical and organisational measures in such a manner that processing will meet the requirements of the GDPR and ensure the protection of the rights of the individual[1].

Sufficient guarantees in terms of considering a video conferencing provider may include:

1 Article 28(1) General Data Protection Regulation (EU) 2016/679

- Whether they have sufficient technical expertise to assist you in carrying out your obligations under the GDPR (e.g. relating to technical measures or data breach notification);
- Whether they can provide you with relevant documentation (e.g. can you obtain a copy of their privacy policy from their website?);
- Whether personal information will be stored outside the EEA and, if so, what safeguards are in place for international transfers of data (e.g. is this detailed in their privacy policy on their website?); and
- Whether the provider has security settings which allow you to keep meetings secure (e.g. use of passwords, encryption, ability to control which participants record the meeting).

Once you are satisfied that the video conferencing provider has the capability of providing a secure environment, you will need to ensure there is a contract in place that meets the requirements of the GDPR[2]. This will normally be incorporated into the provider's terms and conditions and may be referred to as a 'data processing agreement' or 'data processing addendum'. Therefore, you should check the provider's terms and conditions and privacy policy to ensure it includes data processing clauses.

You will also need to ensure you correctly implement the security features provided by the video conferencing provider as these may not always be installed automatically. This may include:

- Restricting access to meetings and video calls;
- Removing the meeting ID and password from the meeting title;

---

2 Article 28(3) General Data Protection Regulation (EU) 2016/679

- Using strong passwords to log into accounts; and
- Ensuring the recording function is only available to the meeting organiser.

Data Protection Impact Assessment

In order to assess the security and suitability of a video conferencing provider, you may wish to consider conducting a data protection impact assessment (DPIA).

The GDPR introduced an obligation on Controller's to conduct a DPIA where processing presents a high risk to individuals' interests[3] (this includes large scale public monitoring or if you intend to offer online services directly to children). The use of DPIAs is a key element of ensuring privacy by design and by default and demonstrating accountability for GDPR compliance.

Even if you do not consider the use of video conferencing to present a high risk to the individuals' interests, DPIAs are examples of best practice when implementing new technology and will demonstrate compliance with the GDPR. A DPIA will also address at outset any issues you may face further down the line (e.g. can we record the meetings? How will we comply with subject access requests?) and therefore can save you time in long run.

A DPIA is a process to assess and minimise the data protection risks of a project. It may not be possible to ensure that there is no risk at all to individuals but conducting a DPIA will assist you in minimising the risk to individuals and assessing whether or not the level of risk is acceptable in the circumstances, taking into account the benefits of the technology you want to implement.

3 Article 35 General Data Protection Regulation (EU) 2016/679

There is no standard template to use when conducting a DPIA. The GDPR states that a DPIA that contains at least[4]:

- A systematic description of the envisaged processing operations and the purposes of the processing, including, where applicable, the legitimate interest pursued by the controller;
- An assessment of the necessity and proportionality of the processing operations in relation to the purposes;
- An assessment of the risks to the rights and freedoms of individuals;
- The measures envisaged to address the risks, including safeguards, security measures and mechanisms to ensure the protection of personal data and to demonstrate compliance with the GDPR taking into account the rights and legitimate interests of individuals.

Taking those elements of a DPIA and applying them to the use of video conferencing, we suggest reviewing the following considerations:

- **Description of the processing and the purpose of the processing** – This should be a general description of the use of video conferencing and your reasons for implementing this technology;
- **An assessment of the necessity and proportionality of video conferencing** – In order to assess the necessity and proportionality of video conferencing, you should include details of how you will ensure data protection compliance as this is a good measure of necessity and proportionality. Guidance from the Article 29 Data Protection Working Party (now known as the European

4 Article 35(7) General Data Protection Regulation (EU) 2016/679

Data Protection Board) states that when assessing necessity and proportionality, you should include details of the following[5]:

- Your lawful basis for processing;
- How you will comply with the 'data minimisation' principle;
- How you will provide privacy information to individuals;
- How you will comply with individual rights' requests;
- Measures in place to ensure your data processor complies with data protection law; and
- Safeguards in place for international transfers of data.

• **An assessment of the risks to the rights and freedoms of individuals** – In order to assess the risk video conferencing poses to the rights and freedoms of individuals, it is important to be clear that risk is not limited to fraud or financial loss. It can also include the inability to exercise data protection rights, the loss of control over their personal information, loss of confidentiality, reputational damage and identity theft or fraud[6]. As part of this assessment, you should consider what risk there will be to individuals in the event of a data security breach including unauthorised access to meetings. Common risks posed by video conferencing include:

  - unauthorised third parties gaining access to meetings;
  - 'phishing' attempts by third parties;

---

5 WP29 Guidelines on Data Protection Impact Assessment and determining whether processing is "likely to result in high risk" for the purposes of Regulation 2016/679 (WP248)

6 https://ico.org.uk/for-organisations/guide-to-data-protection/guide-to-the-general-data-protection-regulation-gdpr/data-protection-impact-assessments-dpias/

- inappropriate use of the recording function by staff and participants to the meeting;
- staff not implementing the appropriate security settings on their device; and
- inadvertent display of confidential documents during a video conference.

- **Measures in place to mitigate the risks that you have identified** – Once you have identified the risks posed by video conferencing, you should then identify what measures you can put in place to mitigate against each of the risks identified. This may include:
  - Deciding that certain meetings are unsuitable to be held via video conference;
  - Taking additional security measures;
  - Providing additional training to staff to ensure they know how to apply the correct security settings;
  - Preparing internal guidance or protocols;
  - Amending your privacy notices, record of processing activity and data protection policies to include reference to video conferencing;
  - Ensuring participants are able to object to meetings being recorded (e.g. are given the opportunity to turn their camera/microphone off).

Once your DPIA has been completed, the measures you propose to mitigate against the identified risks should be implemented and recorded on the DPIA. The DPIA should then be kept under review, particularly where the use of technology is involved, as practices and technology will change rapidly over time and technical security measures are likely to become outdated quickly.

Recording of Meetings

Many video conferencing providers have the function to record meetings. However, just because you have the ability to record the meeting does not mean that you should. Consideration should be given primarily to the need to record the meeting in the first place. If you would not record the meeting in the office, consider why it is now necessary to record the virtual meeting and whether or not meeting minutes would suffice. There are circumstances where recording meetings is sensible (e.g. a training course that can be circulated to other members of staff) but these should be considered on a case by case basis as there are data protection implications where meetings are recorded.

If it is necessary to record a meeting, participants should be made aware that the meeting will be recorded at the outset so that individuals have the ability to turn their camera and/or microphone off if they choose to do so. Security settings should also be configured to ensure that only the meeting organiser has the ability to record the meeting. This will avoid multiple copies of the recording being held and reduces the risk of information recorded in the meeting being used for unauthorised purposes.

If a meeting is recorded, it should be stored centrally on your system (e.g. as opposed to on staff's own devices) so that the recording is kept under the control of the Controller. This is important as recording of meetings may be requested by individuals as part of a subject access request and therefore you will need to be able to search the recordings in the event such a request is received.

You will also need to consider how long the recording will be kept for. Neither the GDPR nor the Data Protection Act 2018 provide specific timescales for how long personal information should be kept for. You will need to consider your reasons why you need to keep a recording and be able to justify the period of time you will keep the recording for. Remember that keeping personal information 'just in case' you may need it at a later date is not a sufficient justification for retaining personal information[7].

Summary

To summarise, prior to selecting a new video conferencing provider or reviewing your existing video conferencing provider, you should take the following steps in order to demonstrate compliance with data protection law:

1. Can the video conferencing provider give sufficient guarantees as to their own GDPR compliance?
2. Have they provided a data processing contract which complies with the terms of the GDPR?
3. Do they store personal information outside the EEA? If so, what safeguards are in place to permit international transfer of personal data under the GDPR?
4. What security features do you need to activate prior to using the video conferencing technology?
5. Have you completed a Data Protection Impact Assessment to assess the risks to individuals and identify the measures you need to put in place to mitigate those risks?

---

7 https://ico.org.uk/for-organisations/guide-to-data-protection/guide-to-the-general-data-protection-regulation-gdpr/principles/storage-limitation

6. Do you need to update your data protection compliance documents such as privacy notices, data protection policies and records of processing activities?

7. Do your staff need any additional training on the use of video conferencing?

CHAPTER FOURTEEN MONITORING HOME AND AGILE WORKING

In this Chapter:

- What counts as monitoring?
- What are the data protection considerations applicable to monitoring?
- Is monitoring the same as interception of communications?
- How does the law apply to monitoring of home and agile workers?
- Summary

As discussed in Chapter 5 (Supervision and Management of Homeworkers) the management of home and agile workers can be challenging due to the lack of visibility of their activity and their potentially different working schedules.

Considering the organisation's own commercial and information security interests and the wellbeing of employees there may be several reasons for the organisation wanting to know what its remote workers are doing and how they are doing it.

What Counts as Monitoring?

The law and guidance applicable to monitoring cover a wide range of activities that organisations often undertake. There is no statutory definition of "monitoring". The ICO's Employment Practices Code covers monitoring in Part 3 and defines it as:

> *Activities that set out to collect information about workers by keeping them under some form of observation, normally with a view to checking their performance or conduct. This could be done directly, indirectly, perhaps by examining their work output, or by electronic means.*

The ICO and EDPB guidance on monitoring give a number of examples of what would fall within this broad classification and they include:

- information gathered from business systems such as sales systems, CRM systems and document management systems,
- video or audio recording or live surveillance,
- checking emails and voicemails (live or by accessing stored data),
- examining activity logs in software such as browsers and cloud-based applications,
- data loss prevention (DLP) software which scans outgoing and incoming emails,
- TLS interception (where the email system opens encrypted messages before they are released to users to check their contents),

- mobile device management on devices provided by the organisation and those belonging to the affected individuals (see Chapter 13 for more on Bring Your Own Device working) and
- taking information from social media accounts (e.g. to monitor compliance with contractual restrictions or to assess absences from work).

Monitoring is not prohibited either by the GDPR and Data Protection Act or (where it applies) by RIPA. That is not to say that organisations can declare open season on excessive and unjustified monitoring of home and agile workers any more than they can in a traditional workplace.

The important assessment for the organisation to make is whether the benefit it can gain from the monitoring it proposes is sufficient to justify the intrusion into the private life or communications of the affected individuals.

Monitoring is a classic example of an activity that should be subject to a Data Protection Impact Assessment. For more on the legal requirements and best practice for these see Chapter 17.

What Are the Data Protection Considerations Applicable to Monitoring?

Monitoring the activity of employees or volunteers wherever they are working is an example of processing their personal data and the GDPR and Data Protection Act will apply to it.

The ICO's guidance has established for a long time that performance information that has consequences for an individual would be that individual's personal data even if the individual's name or image does not appear in it. The position is even clearer if what is being monitored includes email or other communications created by the individual personally because those materials are personal data because they show activity and probably contain the individual's name or other identifying features and because they will contain expressions of the individual's opinions.

The ICO Employment Practices Code has not been updated since the GDPR came into effect although it is considered by the ICO to provide guidance that remains applicable. The EDPB Opinion on data processing at work in 2017 expressly addressed the terms of GDPR which had been finalised in 2016.

One common theme in both the ICO's Code and the EDPB's Opinion is that the justifiable and lawful extent of monitoring is usually far less than the degree of monitoring that the organisation might be capable of undertaking especially given recent developments in analytics. Another repeated point is that monitoring involving personal data and so engaging the Data Protection Act may not be necessary to achieve what the organisation needs and so should not be an automatic choice.

The ICO's Code contains guidance on how to assess any planned monitoring to determine whether it would be appropriate. The suggested steps (with some added examples) are:

1. Identify clearly the purpose and likely benefits of the monitoring, for example
    - is it to maintain the security of systems and the personal data of others?
    - is it for the organisation's commercial benefit in managing performance and efficiency?
2. Identify any likely adverse impact such as
    - intrusion into the private lives and communications of individuals

- personal data being seen by those in the organisation with no legitimate need to see it
- impact on the trust and confidence between the organisation and the remote worker
- oppressive or demeaning levels of monitoring.

3. Consider alternatives to monitoring which might include
   - training and communication rather than systemic monitoring
   - reactive examination of stored information rather than continuous monitoring
   - spot checks or automated monitoring to reduce the instances of other individuals seeing personal data, especially on an ongoing basis.
4. Address the compliance obligations that arise from monitoring such as
   - the requirement to inform data subjects about the nature extent and purpose of any processing of their personal data[1]
   - maintaining the purpose for which monitoring data are intended to be processed and not using the data for other purposes unless strictly justified[2]

1 GDPR Article 13 on privacy notices requires this and other information to be made available at the point of first acquisition of data.

2 GDPR Article 5(1)(b) – the "purpose limitation" principle

- how to manage subject access[3] or other individual rights requests[4] in relation to the monitoring data.

The legitimate expectation of individuals to privacy and home life (as set out in Article 8 of the European Convention on Human Rights) should always be a factor in considering any monitoring and should only be overridden to the extent that it is a necessary means of achieving the organisation's legitimate objective.

Organisations should be clear in their assessments which of the lawful grounds for processing they intend to use for monitoring, especially if the monitoring relates to special category data such as health or trade union information[5].

Both the ICO and EDPB are clear that consent is highly unlikely ever to be a legitimate ground for monitoring, especially in a work context. That is because to be valid under GDPR, consent must be "freely given" and capable of being withdrawn[6]. In an employment context the imbalance of power between the parties is considered to be such that an employee cannot give consent freely. If the organisation considers the monitoring to be necessary it will have to establish that on a non-consensual basis.

For normal personal data Article 6 of GDPR is applicable and the most likely options are where the processing is necessary for:

- the performance of a contract to which the data subject is a party (i.e. the employment contract)[7],

---

3 GDPR Article 15 on subject access rights

4 For example, the right to erasure (right to be forgotten), the right to rectification of data, the right to restriction of processing or the right to object to processing including profiling and automated decision-making.

5 For the full list of special category data see GDPR article 9(1)

6 GDPR Article 7(3) and (4)

7 GDPR Article 6(1)(b)

- compliance with a legal obligation to which the controller is subject (e.g. requirements under legislation relating to employment and taxation and the requirements of the Data Protection Act)[8],
- a task carried out in the public interest or in the exercise of official authority (applicable to public bodies)[9], or
- the purposes of the legitimate interests pursued by the controller or by a third party, <u>except where such interests are overridden by the interests or fundamental rights and freedoms of the data subject</u> which require protection of personal data...(the "legitimate interests" ground is not available to public bodies)[10].

The emphasis is added above to make clear that even if the monitoring is aligned with a legitimate interest of an organisation it is still unlawful if it is too intrusive.

For special category personal data there are stricter and narrower grounds for processing. Organisations should try not to process special category data in monitoring wherever possible because the compliance requirements and likely consequences of any data breach are higher for this kind of data.

Article 9 of GDPR contains the lawful ground for processing special category data and potential grounds for monitoring remote workers could be:

- processing is necessary for the purposes of carrying out the obligations...of the controller...in the field of employment... law...[11],

---

8 GDPR Article 6(1)(c)

9 GDPR Article 6(1)(e)

10 GDPR Article 6(1)(f)

11 GDPR Article 9(1)(b)

- processing relates to personal data manifestly made public by the data subject (e.g. social media)[12],
- processing is necessary for the purposes of preventive or occupational medicine, for the assessment of the working capacity of the employee…[13].

If a ground for processing is applicable to the planned monitoring, the organisation as the data controller then has to make sure that it acts within the data protection principles and respects the rights of data subjects.

Where monitoring activity involving personal data is justified, it should be done to the most limited extent possible in order to comply with the data protection principles including fairness in processing[14] and data minimisation[15]. Quality control is essential in order to satisfy the accuracy principle[16] and there must be a plan for how long the information gained from monitoring will be retained for no longer than necessary[17] and how it will be kept safe from "unauthorised or unlawful processing and against accidental loss, destruction or damage"[18].

Even if home working or agile working is not planned to be permanent, if it going to be monitored then the Data Protection Act and GDPR apply and organisations as data controllers will be expected to comply or face enforcement and potential liability.

---

12 GDPR Article 9(1)(e)

13 GDPR Article 9(1)(h)

14 GDPR Article 5(1)(a)

15 GDPR Article 5(1)(c)

16 GDPR Article 5(1)(d)

17 GDPR Article 5(1)(e) "storage limitation" principle

18 GDPR Article 5(1)(f) "integrity and confidentiality" principle – usually known as the "data security principle"

Is Monitoring the Same as Interception of Communications?

"Interception of communications" sounds like something reserved for the secret service or at least the police and the intention of IPA is to regulate phone tapping, email interception and obtaining communications data. That means that the legislation defines interception, restricts when it should happen and creates some exemptions from that general rule though parts of IPA and the IP Regulations.

The ICO Employment Practices Code in its supplementary documents includes guidance for data controllers to help them assess whether what they are planning on doing is "interception of communications" with reference to the previous legislation under the Regulation of Investigatory Powers Act 2000 and the Telecommunications (Lawful Business Practice)(Interception of Communications) Regulations 2000.

The IPA sets out the office of unlawful interception in section 3(1) which says:

> A person commits an offence if—
>
> (a) the person intentionally intercepts a communication in the course of its transmission by means of—
>
> (i) a public telecommunication system,
>
> (ii) a private telecommunication system, or
>
> (iii) a public postal service,
>
> (b) the interception is carried out in the United Kingdom, and
>
> (c) the person does not have lawful authority to carry out the interception.

To explain how part (a) of the offence works, the IPA defines "interception" and the two elements of it are firstly that the person modifies or monitors communications through or with the telecommunication system and secondly that the effect of that is to make any content of the communication available to a person who is not the sender or intended recipient during transmission or at any time when the communication is stored in the system[19]. The IPA applies to interceptions done by way of recording at that time with the communication available to a person afterwards[20].

That latter element is a change from the previous legislation and makes elements of the ICO Employment Practices Code guidance obsolete.

Examples of interception in the course of transmission could include:

- a supervisor listening in on calls as they happen,
- emails stored on a server before the intended recipient has opened them and
- an email system that automatically opens outgoing and incoming emails and attachments to check for viruses (whether via the email system or the wireless network connecting users' computers to it).

If the planned monitoring would be interception of communications the next step is to assess the potential for getting outside the defined criminal offence into the law types of interception.

There is no offence under section 3 if interception in a private telecommunications system is done by a person with a right to control opera-

19 IPA section 4(1), 4(2), 4(3) and 4(4).

20 IPA section 4(5).

tion or use of that system (or someone acting with that person's consent)[21].

The next option is to establish "Lawful authority" for the purposes of section 3(1)(c) of the IPA. This can be done in a number of ways and the most relevant for work-relate monitoring is if sections 44 to 52 of the IPA give that authority[22].

Consent of the sender and recipient can be a solution[23]. As the ICO guidance rightly observes in relation to the similar provision in the previous legislation that while it may be possible to inform a person making a call to an organisation and infer consent from the call continuing it will be far harder to get consent from the sender of an email to an organisation and in this setting relying on consent as a compliance solution is riskier than finding a better option.

The most likely solution is in section 46 of the IPA which allows for Regulations permitting interceptions in connection with relevant activities which include "any business"[24] as well as government departments, public authorities and office holders[25].

In the IP Regulations made under IPA section 46 there is a three-part test to establish whether conduct is authorised for the purposes of the IPA and all three parts must be satisfied[26]. The three parts are:

---

21 IPA section 3(2)

22 IPA section 6(1)(b).

23 IPA section 44(1).

24 IPA section 46(4)(a) and the title of section 46 is "Interception by businesses etc. for monitoring and record-keeping purposes" suggesting the business monitoring is clearly intended to be possible.

25 IPA section 46(4).

26 IP Regulations regulation 3(1)(a) to (c).

(1) there is interception of a communication in the course of transmission by means of a telecommunications system which happens with the express consent of the system controller[27]; and

(2) the conduct is one of

(a) monitoring or keeping a record of communications for a range of reasons including establishing the existence of facts[28], ascertaining compliance with regulatory requirements[29], ascertaining or demonstrating standards expected of users[30], investigating or detecting unauthorised system use[31] and securing effective operation of the system[32],

(b) monitoring communications to determine whether they are relevant to the "relevant activity" (i.e. the operation of the business or public authority)[33] or

(c) monitoring in a confidential counselling or support service in which users may remain anonymous (which allows for support to call-handlers)[34] and

(3) the interception is to monitor or keep a record relating to the system controller's relevant activities[35] and is in a system provided for use in those activities[36] and the system controller

---

27 IP Regulations regulation 3(1)(a).

28 IP Regulations regulation 3(2)(a).

29 IP Regulations regulation 3(2)(b).

30 IP Regulations regulation 3(2)(c).

31 IP Regulations regulation 3(2)(f).

32 IP Regulations regulation 3(2)(g).

33 IP Regulations regulation 3(3).

34 IP Regulations regulation 3(4).

35 IP Regulations regulation 4(1)(a).

36 IP Regulations regulation 4(1)(b).

has made all reasonable efforts to inform users that communications in that system may be intercepted[37].

It is important for organisations to make sure that they are on the right side of the IPA and IP Regulations because the consequences of a breach can include monetary penalties imposed by the Investigatory Powers Commissioner[38] and civil liability for claims by the sender or intended recipient of the unlawfully-intercepted communication[39].

Interception of communications is a complex and contentious area of law and has other aspects that are beyond the scope of this book (such as giving access to business systems to assist the prevention or detection of crime or in relation to national security). Any organisation considering whether it is acting lawfully within IPA and the IP Regulations should take specialist advice and make sure that it has appropriate documentation of its decisions, procedures and management arrangements.

It is important to remember that if monitoring is lawful under the IPA, that does not affect the application of GDPR and the Data Protection Act to the way in which the resulting data are processed. Similarly, meeting the requirements of the Data Protection Act and GDPR in relation to monitoring may not be sufficient to achieve compliance with the IPA.

How Does the Law Apply to Monitoring of Home and Agile Workers?

Organisations accustomed to having individuals working in an office or other workplace occupied by the organisations have to reconsider their methods to monitoring and assessing individuals who are no longer in that place either regularly or at all.

37 IP Regulations regulation 4(1)(c).

38 IPA section 7 with a maximum of £50,000 (section 7(5)).

39 IPA section 8.

Routine interaction with managers and other colleagues is an unavoidable element of working in a shared space such as an office and many organisations regard punctual attendance at the place of work to be a part of the individual's performance.

Where home or agile working becomes the norm, many of the usual indicators of performance or compliance with requirements cease to apply and organisations need to assess whether different measurements of performance and/or different methods of measurement are needed to achieve effective management. A move to large-scale home or agile working may be accompanied by a change of policy about flexible working and a reduced priority being given to when in the day or the week a person is doing work or the time at which they start or finish[40].

Organisations need to reassess what they want to monitor and why and then assess how that can be done with due consideration for the rights of the affected individuals.

Cases about monitoring in traditional workplaces have considered the extent to which an element of private life should be maintained even when at the employer or other organisation's premises during working hours[41].That assessment is potentially reversed in the case of home working where the question becomes what part of the domestic setting can legitimately be monitored or controlled by the employer or organisation. The EDPB Opinion takes that line and expects a strict assessment of when monitoring of individuals at home is necessary.

It is sensible for organisations to think through their existing or planned monitoring measures to document their assessments of the intended benefits, identified risks to individual rights, mitigation measures and

40 Hours worked may remain relevant to National Minimum Wage Regulations or Working Time Regulations compliance – see Chapter 7.

41 For example human rights cases such as *Copland v United Kingdom* (2007) on emails from business premises, *Halford v United Kingdom* (1997) on telephone calls from business premises and *Barbulescu v Romania* (2016) on use of professional instant messaging services for private correspondence.

compliance actions. They should take the opportunity to consider potential alternatives to systemic monitoring especially if it involves interception of communications.

The EDPB Opinion contains specific reference to monitoring home working[42] and recognises that remote workers will be outside the organisation's usual physical security measures. It considers that reacting to this by deploying keystroke and mouse movement logging, screen capture (randomly or at intervals), application logging and enabling webcams would be disproportionate and very unlikely ever to be justifiable as within the legitimate interests of the data controller under GDPR Article 6(1)(f).

It is a simple question for an organisation to consider: if it did not do this sort of monitoring before Covid-19 why has it become appropriate now? Has home and agile working created such heightened risks of system misuse that this sort of intrusive monitoring is necessary now?

Existing monitoring built into work systems (assuming it is compatible with GDPR and IPA) may be sufficient if home and agile workers will operate by logging into the same systems and creating visible outputs and logged activity as they would have done in an office setting. The degree to which organisations should consider more monitoring for home workers than was the case when they were office workers should be in line with the increase in the risk that the monitoring is intended to address by way of its intended benefits.

For more on the application of data protection principles generally and data security to home working please see Chapters 9 and 10.

Monitoring for example through mobile device management is a consideration in relation to BYOD working methods and for more on this see Chapter 12.

---

42 Opinion 2/2017 on data processing at work, section 5.4.1 "Processing operations resulting from monitoring ICT usage outside the workplace – Monitoring Home and Remote Working"

The capacity to record video conferences exists in popular platforms. Using this would constitute monitoring and potentially interception of communications and organisations should look carefully at how they would justify recording meeting held in Zoom or Teams where meetings in a room at the organisation's offices would not have been subject to audio or video recording. Chapter 13 deals with video conferencing in more detail.

If monitoring is appropriate it is essential then to be clear on what will happen to the data processed as a result of it. Both the ICO and EDPB guidance are clear on the threat to individual rights that is posed by secondary processing. The GDPR requires up-front information on the use to which personal data will be put and the purpose limitation principle states that the data controller should use the data for the stated purpose(s) only. The assessment of monitoring should include clarifying and limiting the purposes and making that limitation known to those who are authorised to access the monitoring data.

The EDPB gives an example of controlled access to a secure storage room. Access logs are kept for the purpose of clarifying who had access to the secure space at the time of any problem in order to investigate it. It would not be appropriate to use the access logs for another purpose such as employee performance evaluation is that use has not been made clear to the affected individuals and they have a chance to address any issues they have with the data being used in that way.

Secondary processing by using monitoring data for profiling or automated decision-making engages individual rights to object as well as the requirement for notification of the purposes of processing. If for example an organisation decides to use system log-in records as an indicator of working patterns it should say it is going to do that and build in a way to discuss the results with individuals before making decisions. As an example, a home worker attending a webinar for work reasons might do that outside the organisation's IT system and so appear not to be working. Equally, a home worker's role might legitimately require doing something offline like reading a book or manual. Furthermore, the expected working pattern should be something addressed in either the home working policy or the individual's contract[43] and different log-in schedules might be entirely in line with what has been agreed.

Summary

Monitoring home and agile workers is data processing in almost all imaginable cases and will be interception of communications in a large number of examples.

Organisations need to assess the issues and risks they are trying to address and what benefits they plan to achieve through monitoring. They can then consider impacts, alternatives and compliance steps to set up their monitoring to be proportionate and in line with the applicable laws.

Monitoring arrangements should be referenced in a number of documents addressed elsewhere in this book including:

- Record of processing (if required under GDPR)
- Home working policy
- Home working contact amendments
- Privacy notices for home and agile workers

Excessive and systemic monitoring is sometimes easier to do than to avoid if technology is deployed with settings and features enabled without a proper assessment of their effect. The ICO and EDPB stress the importance of robust data protection impact assessments and in the event of a dispute with a home or agile worker about monitoring that

43 For discussion of what should be in which document see Chapter 7 (Homeworking contractual provisions and what to include in your homeworking policy).

DPIA would be the first document any advisor or ICO investigator would want to see[44].

44 See Chapter 17 for more detailed treatment of DPIAs.

CHAPTER FIFTEEN
HOMEWORKING AND SUBJECT ACCESS REQUESTS

One of the key aims of the GDPR is to empower individuals and give them control over their personal information. Individuals have a number of rights under the GDPR. These are:

- The right to rectify incorrect personal information;
- The right to access personal information;
- The right to be forgotten;
- The right to transfer personal information to a different organisation;
- The right to object to direct marketing;
- The right to restrict processing of personal information;
- The right to make a complaint to the ICO; and
- The right to not be subject to profiling or automated decision making.

For the purposes of this book, we have concentrated on the right to access personal information, commonly known as a subject access request, as this is the right which we see commonly causes issues where staff are working from home.

What is a Subject Access Request?

Under the GDPR, an individual is entitled to be given a copy of their personal data from an organisation processing their personal information[1]. This is known as a subject access request or SAR. Along with a copy of their personal information, an individual is also entitled to receive information about:

- The reasons or purposes for which their personal information is being processed;
- The type of personal information concerned;
- Who that personal information has been shared with or disclosed to;
- How long their personal information will be held for;
- The source of the information;
- Information about how to make a complaint about how their personal information has been used; and
- If personal information has been transferred outside the European Economic Area, what safeguards are in place to protect their personal data.

For the majority of organisations, a subject access request is most likely to come from a current or former employee or a client or customer. Whilst staff are working from home, it is important that they continue to be able to recognise a SAR. A SAR does not need to be in writing to be valid (e.g. it could be by telephone, letter, e-mail or even via social media). Therefore, a SAR may be sent to a member of staff directly rather than it being sent to the individual or department who would

1 Article 15 General Data Protection Regulation (EU) 2016/679

usually handle a SAR for your organisation. A request is valid even if the individual has not sent it directly to the person who normally deals with such requests. Therefore, it is important to ensure that all staff can recognise a subject access request and treat it appropriately by forwarding it promptly to correct person.

SARs and Home working

Home working poses a number of data protection risks and whilst the majority of these risks relate to security, there is also a risk that individual's rights are impacted if subject access requests are not acknowledged or are not handled correctly.

Where staff are using their own devices rather than equipment issued by the organisation, it can be more difficult to respond to a subject access request if information is stored on the personal device rather than on a central system. You will be unable to guarantee that you will comply with a subject access request if you are not aware of the existence of information as it is stored on a member of staff's personal device rather than on your own central system. Therefore, you should either ensure work is always saved in a central location or ensure your BYOD policy enables you to access the personal device and search it for company information (see 'Use of Personal Devices' above for further information). Having information saved centrally is preferable as it avoids any potential issues that may arise should a member of staff refuse to provide access to the device or deletes all content on the device prior to handing it over.

Staff should also be aware that all e-mails, documents, recordings and instant messages they create containing personal information whilst working from home could have to be disclosed in the event a subject access request is received. Therefore, all documentation created whilst working from home should be treated as being retrievable and staff should avoid saying anything which would cause offence or embarrassment if it was forwarded to colleagues or third parties, or found its way into the public domain.

How you will ensure subject access requests will be properly complied with should form part of your data protection impact assessment when implementing your BYOD policy (see 'Use of Personal Devices' above) and should form part of any training you provide to staff who are working from home.

Summary

To summarise, you will need to make sure you are able to comply with subject access requests regardless of whether or not staff are working at home or in the office and take into account the following considerations:

1. Are staff aware of how to recognise a subject access request? Do they know who a subject access request should be sent to within your organisation?

2. Are staff aware that all documentation they create (including recordings of meetings) whilst working at home may have to be disclosed in the event a subject access request is received?

3. Does your BYOD policy cover where information is to be stored so that it can be searched in the event of a subject access request?

4. Does your data protection impact assessment for implementing BYOD cover how you will comply with subject access requests?

5. Do your staff need any further training?

CHAPTER SIXTEEN
HOME WORKING, GDPR AND VICARIOUS LIABILITY

In this section:

- What is vicarious liability?
- How does vicarious liability apply to Data Protection?
- How does vicarious liability apply to home and agile working?

The concept of vicarious liability has recently been assessed in the Supreme Court in its application to UK data protection legislation and misuse of information. Increased levels of home and agile working add another element to the question with greater numbers of people working with reduced degrees of oversight, mobile phones and remote access to IT systems. The risks of infringements of GDPR and the Data Protection Act during home and agile working are addressed in several chapters of this book and the prospects of liability coming back to the organisation must be assessed as part of overall risk management and policy setting.

What is Vicarious Liability?

This legal term refers to the rules which govern when one party is legally responsible in law (i.e. liable) for the conduct of another party.

In an organisational setting this can include assessing whether employers are liable for the conduct of employees and whether charities should be liable for the conduct of volunteers.

As discussed further below, in the context of data protection the employees of a data controller are not usually treated as separate data controllers and are instead treated as part of the corporate data controller. Where an employee goes outside that usual analysis the issue of vicarious liability can arise, especially as the reason for being outside the usual analysis is likely to involve some misconduct.

How Does Vicarious Liability Apply to Data Protection?

This question was recently addressed by the UK Supreme Court in the case of *WM Morrison Supermarkets plc v Various Claimants*[1].

The claim against Morrisons was made by over nine thousand of its employees following a serious data breach affecting their payroll information. The breach was caused by the deliberate actions of a rogue employee acting out of malice against the company as a result of a previous disciplinary decision.

That employee was given payroll information in the usual course of his role and communicated it to external auditors as instructed. He retained an unauthorised copy and disclosed the payroll information of 98,998 other staff to a file sharing website using masking software via an email account linked to a pay as you go (or "burner") mobile phone created in an attempt to frame a colleague. He also sent the data on discs to several newspapers.

The offending employee was tried and imprisoned for a number of offences with sentences totalling over eight years. The immediate response to the disclosure cost Morrisons £2.26m.

Some of the affected employees joined together to make claims directly against Morrisons alleging breach by it of the Data Protection Act 1998 as well as misuse of information and breach of confidentiality and also

---

1 UK Supreme Court judgment given on 1 April 2020.

claims against Morrisons on the basis that it was vicariously liable for the actions of the offending employee.

In the initial High Court decision on liability, the Court held that Morrisons was not primarily liable (i.e. it did nothing wrong itself) and that it was vicariously liable for the offending employee's actions under the Data Protection Act 1998 and otherwise. That decision was upheld by the Court of Appeal and then came to the Supreme Court on a further appeal by Morrisons.

The Supreme Court reviewed the cases about vicarious liability and considered how they apply to this case and to organisations' liability under the Data Protection legislation.

On the question of vicarious liability the Supreme Court decided unanimously that on the facts Morrisons should not be liable for the actions of the offending employee. That was the case not because his actions were criminal offences but because they were not closely enough connected to the performance of his duties as an employee for liability to arise. The Court gave a summary of the key principles of vicarious liability which are outlined in the next section below.

The Supreme Court did consider the arguments advanced by Morrisons that the data protection legislation excludes the possibility of vicarious liability for the duties created by the legislation and for other claims relating to misuse of private information.

The case involved an analysis that the offending employee became by his conduct a separate data controller rather than being seen as an employee of the primary data controller acting within its usual operations. This is a significant distinction in the case because in most cases of employees causing data breaches or other infringement of the data protection legislation are not assessed as independent controllers so the question of vicarious liability does not arise. In this case Morrisons as the primary data controller was found not to have contravened the data protection legislation. For it to be liable to the employees it would have to bear responsibility for the offending employee's actions when he acted as a separate controller.

The Court considered that there was nothing in the data protection legislation to justify disapplying usual English legal rules such as vicarious liability and that while the legislation did (and the GDPR still does) set out a specific right on the part of the victim of an infringement of rights to make a claim against the data controller that should not be read as removing other possible ways of making a claim such as seeking to establish vicarious liability of one controller for the actions of a second controller. As in the Morrisons case there would have been little point making claims against the imprisoned former employee who would most likely have no insurance for the liability or assets sufficient to cover many thousands of claims.

The key point from this case for data controllers is that they can be vicariously liable for the actions of another data controller if the circumstances are sufficient to justify applying the vicarious liability rules.

How Does Vicarious Liability Apply to Home and Agile Working?

As noted above, in most cases of an organisational data controller with employees, liability resulting from the actions or omissions of the employee are normally assessed within the primary liability of the data controller/employer and so questions of the adequacy of training, policies and supervision come into play.

There remain circumstances in which an individual might be treated as having acted as a separate data controller and in those cases the question is whether there is a sufficiently close connection between their actions and their employment or other role for vicarious liability to be justified[2].

2 In the *Morrisons* case the Supreme Court referenced the judgment of its predecessor the House of Lords in *Dubai Aluminium Co Ltd v Salaam* in 2002 as stating the "close connection" test correctly.

It is the relationship between the two parties and the objective of the second party's actions that create the potential for vicarious liability rather than their respective locations. Organisations cannot safely assume that if an individual is working from home that employee or volunteer cannot create various liability on the part of the organisation by acting in a manner that results in their being assessed as a separate data controller. The capacity in which a person acts and their objective is much more significant for assessing vicarious liability than their whereabouts at the time.

If the organisation has required the individual to work at home or in another location not occupied by the organisation that will make vicarious liability a serious possibility depending on the other facts in each case. Requiring home or agile working is no different to requiring work from a hotel, conference centre or customer's premises: if the individual is where the organisation requires or expects the individual to be or the organisation accepts or tolerates a place of work adopted by the individual then being away from a previous or conventional workplace will not of itself defeat a claim of vicarious liability.

The key question in the assessment of vicarious liability is whether the individual is acting in the discharge of what the organisation requires or in the interest of the organisation in a way that shows the necessary close connection.

Another case involving Morrisons was discussed in the recent case as an example of where vicarious liability for criminal actions would apply. In that other case[3], an employee in a petrol station kiosk decided inappropriately to eject a customer and attacked him. The key difference between that criminal conduct and the offending employee's mishandling of colleagues' data was that the employee in the *Mohamud* case was acting within the remit of his job and purportedly advancing his employer's interests, however badly he did it. The employee in the more

3 *Mohamud v WM Morrison Supermarkets plc* decided by the House of Lords in 2016.

recent case did what he did out of hostility to Morrisons and with the intention of damaging it.

The risk for organisations lies in employees misunderstanding their roles and obligations, overstepping what was really required of them and doing a version of their jobs badly. In that sort of case the employer would be at serious risk of vicarious liability existing if the employee's actions are sufficient to make them a separate data controller.

Using equipment provided by an employer does not always result in vicarious liability. In a case involving a police officer using a service weapon in what the house of Lords called "a personal vendetta" it was noted that the officer's actions "had nothing whatever to do with any police duties, either actually or ostensibly"[4]. That was seen as directly applicable in the recent *Morrisons* case because the employee had received the data about colleagues in a legitimate employment context and went on to misuse it.

In a home or agile working scenario, if an employee has equipment provided by the organisation the question of vicarious liability for actions as a separate data controller will not be determined by whether the actions used that equipment or not. A poorly-judged BYOD[5] action connected with an attempt to advance the organisation's interests or to do the home worker's job could result in vicarious liability. The employee in the recent *Morrisons* case did use a work laptop and memory stick at some stages in his actions and vicarious liability did not arise.

There is a criminal offence under the Data Protection Act of unauthorised access to or disclosure of personal data[6]. That is capable of being committed by an individual person misusing access granted in the

---

4 *Attorney General of the British Virgin Islands v Hartwell* decided by the judicial committee of the Privy Council (the House of Lords acting as the appeal court from a Commonwealth jurisdiction) in 2004.

5 Bring Your Own Device (for more on which see Chapter 12)

6 Data Protection Act section 170 (previously Data Protection Act 1998 section 55).

course of employment. One of the considerations for data controllers having to report a data breach to the ICO is whether it is appropriate to name a specific employee as having committed this offence in causing the breach for example by abusing access to IT systems. By reporting the commission of the "unauthorised access" offence the organisation would be flagging the absence of authorisation and suggesting that the conduct was not endorsed or permitted.

As with other aspects of GDPR and Data Protection Act compliance in relation to home working and agile working the best approach for organisations is to plan ahead to reduce the risk of a vicarious liability problem arising. Making clear what the home or agile worker is expected to do (and equally importantly not do) with personal data accessible to them is a sensible approach. If home or agile workers make mistakes in the performance of their roles that is unlikely even to qualify for separate data controller treatment. The best way to reduce liability in that sort of case is to be able to point to appropriate training, policies and awareness which may be sufficient to demonstrate that the organisation had done as much as it could to prevent a breach or infringement.

CHAPTER SEVENTEEN
THE IMPORTANCE OF DATA PROTECTION IMPACT ASSESSMENTS

The speed in which organisations were required to facilitate home working for large proportions of the workforce in response to the Covid-19 crisis was unprecedented. Organisations rose to that challenge and many have found that the benefits of home working mean that they will continue to permit home working in the long term. As we now get used to this new way of working, it is important we now assess the security and risks posed by home working and to address any issues that may have arisen during the initial implementation of home working. It is important that any 'quick fixes' which were put in place to immediately respond to the crisis are assessed properly and consider whether these measures are appropriate in the long term.

The GDPR introduced an obligation on Controller's to conduct a DPIA where processing presents a high risk to individuals' interests[1] (this includes large scale public monitoring or if you intend to offer online services directly to children). The use of DPIAs is a key element of ensuring privacy by design and by default and demonstrating accountability for GDPR compliance.

Even if you do not consider your organisation's home working practices to present a high risk to the individuals' interests, DPIAs are examples of best practice when implementing new technology and will demonstrate compliance with the GDPR. A DPIA will also address at outset any issues you may face further down the line (e.g. can we ensure staff comply with our data protection policies? How will we monitor data

---

1 Article 35 General Data Protection Regulation (EU) 2016/679

breaches? How will we comply with subject assess requests) and therefore can save you time in the long run.

A DPIA is a process to assess and minimise the data protection risks of a project. It may not be possible to ensure that there is no risk at all to individuals but conducting a DPIA will assist you in minimising the risk to individuals and assessing whether or not the level of risk is acceptable in the circumstances, taking into account the benefits of the technology you want to implement.

There is no standard template to use when conducting a DPIA. The GDPR states that a DPIA that contains at least[2]:

- A systematic description of the envisaged processing operations and the purposes of the processing, including, where applicable, the legitimate interest pursued by the controller;
- An assessment of the necessity and proportionality of the processing operations in relation to the purposes;
- An assessment of the risks to the rights and freedoms of individuals;
- The measures envisaged to address the risks, including safeguards, security measures and mechanisms to ensure the protection of personal data and to demonstrate compliance with the GDPR taking into account the rights and legitimate interests of individuals.

Taking those elements of a DPIA and applying them to home working, we suggest reviewing the following considerations:

- **Description of the processing and the purpose of the processing** – This should be a general description of your home

2 Article 35(7) General Data Protection Regulation (EU) 2016/679

working policy and your reasons for implementing this method of working;

- **An assessment of the necessity and proportionality of home working** – In order to assess the necessity and proportionality of home working, you should include details of how you will ensure data protection compliance as this is a good measure of necessity and proportionality. Guidance from the Article 29 Data Protection Working Party (now known as the European Data Protection Board) states that when assessing necessity and proportionality, you should include details of the following[3]:
  - Your lawful basis for processing;
  - How you will comply with the 'data minimisation' principle;
  - How you will comply with the 'purpose limitation' principle;
  - How you will comply with the 'storage limitation' principle';
  - How you will provide privacy information to individuals;
  - How you will comply with individual rights' requests;
  - Measures in place to ensure any data processors you choose to assist with your home working technology complies with data protection law; and
  - Safeguards in place for international transfers of data.

3 WP29 Guidelines on Data Protection Impact Assessment and determining whether processing is "likely to result in high risk" for the purposes of Regulation 2016/679 (WP248)

- **An assessment of the risks to the rights and freedoms of individuals** – In order to assess the risks home working poses to the rights and freedoms of individuals, it is important to be clear that risk is not limited to fraud or financial loss. It can also include the inability to exercise data protection rights, the loss of control over their personal information, loss of confidentiality, reputational damage and identity theft or fraud[4]. As part of this assessment, you should consider what risk there will be to individuals in the event of a data security breach. Common risks posed by home working include:
    - unauthorised third parties gaining access to company devices;
    - 'phishing' attempts by third parties;
    - inappropriate use of business information by staff;
    - staff not implementing the appropriate security settings on their devices; and
    - confidentiality breaches.

- **Measures in place to mitigate the risks that you have identified** – Once you have identified the risks posed by home working, you should then identify what measures you can put in place to mitigate against each of the risks identified. This may include:
    - Deciding that certain business functions are unsuitable to be performed at home;
    - Taking additional security measures;

4 https://ico.org.uk/for-organisations/guide-to-data-protection/guide-to-the-general-data-protection-regulation-gdpr/data-protection-impact-assessments-dpias/

- Providing additional training to staff to ensure they know how to comply with your data protection policy whilst working from home;
- Preparing internal guidance or protocols;
- Amending your privacy notices, record of processing activity and data protection policies to include reference to home working.

Once your DPIA has been completed, the measures you propose to mitigate against the identified risks should be implemented and recorded on the DPIA. The DPIA should then be kept under review, particularly where the use of technology is involved, as practices and technology will change rapidly over time and technical security measures are likely to become outdated quickly.

DPIAs are also likely to be required for different elements of your home working policy (e.g. for video conferencing or the use of Bring Your Own Device). You may wish to conduct separate DPIAs for each of these elements or you may include it in one complete DPIA assessing all the different elements of your home working policy. For further details of what should be considered within these different elements, please see *'Use of Personal Devices'* and *'Video Conferencing'* below.

A template homeworking DPIA has been included at Appendix B of this book.

APPENDIX A
DATA SECURITY IN THE HOME ENVIRONMENT CHECKLIST

The following checklist has been devised to outline the key areas for consideration and any technical and organisational measures that should be implemented for homeworkers in order to manage the potential data protection risks posed by home or agile working.

Ref	Action Title	Action	Status/Date Completed
1.	Accountability and Governance	Make senior management or leadership teams aware of potential risk a lack of compliance with the GDPR could have in respect of homeworking.	
2.	Accountability and Governance	Conduct a data protection impact assessment (DPIA) for homeworking which links to your existing risk management and project management processes.	
3.	Disposal of Confidential Waste	Assess whether you have a procedure in place for handling and disposing of confidential waste in the home environment.	
4.	IT Security	Assess whether you are using the most up to date version of the technological solution to remotely access your systems and networks	

Ref	Action Title	Action	Status/Date Completed
5.	IT Security	Assess whether you can introduce multi-factor authentication to remotely access your systems and networks.	
6.	IT Security	Ensure staff use unique and complex passwords and are aware of the risks of 'phishing'.	
7.	IT Security	If using BYOD, assess whether you can segregate personal use of the device from business use.	
8.	Record and Legal Basis of Processing	Assess whether your Record of Processing Activity in accordance with Article 30 of the GDPR needs to be updated and make any necessary amendments.	
9.	Data Compliance Policies and Procedures	Review your data protection policies, procedures and associated documents to determine whether they need updating or new policies drafting.	
10.	Data Compliance Policies and Procedures	Assess whether BYOD policy is required and, if so, whether there is an appropriate policy document in place to govern the use of work mobile devices such as laptops or mobiles.	
11.	Data Compliance Policies and Procedures	Assess whether your IT security and Acceptable Use policies require updating to reflect the changes in working practice.	

Ref	Action Title	Action	Status/Date Completed
12.	Data Compliance Policies and Procedures	Ensure any new and updated policies, procedures and guidance are communicated to all staff.	
13.	Fair and Transparent Processing	Review your external facing privacy notice and assess whether it needs to be amended to include different methods of communication (e.g. via video conference).	
14.	Fair and Transparent Processing	Review your staff privacy notice and assess whether it needs to be amended to include different methods of communication (e.g. via video conference).	
15.	Breach Response Management	Assess whether data breach procedure has been devised and implemented to ensure data breaches can be reported whilst staff are working remotely.	
16.	Breach Response Management	Ensure data breaches are recorded and monitored to identify trends and prevent re-occurrence.	
17.	Data Subject Rights and Procedures	Ensure there are procedures in place for handling requests from data subjects under the GDPR received whilst working remotely.	
18.	Training and Awareness	Ensure staff are provided with training and guidance following the implementation of new policies and procedures.	

APPENDIX B HOMEWORKING DPIA TEMPLATE

[INSERT COMPANY NAME] HOMEWORKING DATA PROTECTION IMPACT ASSESSMENT

Background

When implementing new projects, initiatives or policies and procedures, the impact of the collection, use and disclosure of any personal information must be considered in light of an individual's right to privacy. Carrying out a data protection impact assessment (DPIA) is a way in which this impact can be assessed.

A DPIA is a process which helps an organisation to identify and reduce the privacy risks of a project, initiative or new policies and procedures. An effective DPIA will be used throughout the development and implementation of a project, using existing project management processes. A DPIA enables an organisation to systematically and thoroughly analyse how a particular project or systems will affect the privacy of the individuals involved.

Homeworking DPIA

We recognise the need for staff to work in a more flexible way which can bring advantages to staff and to the organisation. However, the increased flexibility will involve introducing new technological and organisational measures to ensure staff can work productively out of the office.

In accordance with guidance from the Information Commissioner's Office, a DPIA is being carried out to assess the data protection risks involved in homeworking and identify remedial steps to ensure the protection of personal information and demonstrate compliance with the General Data Protection Regulation (EU) 2016/679 ('the GDPR').

How to start?

You should identify a lead person who is best placed to coordinate and carry out the DPIA process (for example your Data Protection Officer). Consultation with managers and staff is likely to also be required.

1. Data Protection Impact Assessment

1.1 Background Information

Project Name	*[E.g. Introduction of homeworking policy]*
Organisation	
Lead person conducting DPIA	
Job Title	
Date Completed	
Telephone	
E-mail address	
Project Outline – What is being planned?	[*e.g. Implementation of new homeworking policy*]
Purposes / Objectives – Why is it being undertaken?	[*e.g. There has been a significant increase in homeworking in response to the coronavirus pandemic. Homeworking provides staff with flexibility and allows us to put social distancing measures in place.*]

What are the potential privacy impacts of this proposal – how will this change impact individual?	[*e.g. There are increased security risks working outside the office which need to be mitigated.*]
Who is involved in the project? List all stakeholders, internal/external organisations and groups involved.	

1.2 Personal Data Involved

What personal data is being collected, shared or used?	Yes	No	Justifications – is all data required or could some be removed without comprising the project?
Personal details (i.e. name, address, DOB, sex, gender)	☐	☐	
Contact details (i.e. telephone numbers, email address, NOK)	☐	☐	
Information relating to the individual's physical or mental health or condition	☐	☐	
Information relating to the individual's sexual life	☐	☐	
Information relating to the family of the individual and their lifestyle and social circumstances	☐	☐	
Information relating to any criminal offences or alleged offences	☐	☐	

Information relating to criminal proceedings and sentences regarding the individual	☐	☐	
Information which relates to the education and any professional training of the individual	☐	☐	
Information relating to an individual's career and employment history	☐	☐	
Information relating to the financial affairs of the individual	☐	☐	
Information relating to the individual's religion or other beliefs	☐	☐	

1.3 Identify the privacy and related risks

Use this section to identify the key privacy risks and associated compliance and organisational risk.

No.	Privacy Issue	Risk to individual	Compliance risk	Organisational risk
E.g.	*Accessing our systems remotely*	*Remote access could be compromised by malicious third parties*	*Non-compliance with data protection principles – integrity & confidentiality*	*1. Reputational damage 2. Regulatory action / sanction from ICO*
E.g.	*Use of staff's personal devices*	*Devices may not be as secure as work issued equipment*	*Non-compliance with data protection principles – integrity & confidentiality*	*1. Reputational damage 2. Regulatory action / sanction from ICO*
E.g.	*Use of staff's personal devices*	*Information may be stored outside of the company's system resulting in a loss of control of the information.*	*Non-compliance with data protection principles – fair, lawful & transparent processing*	*1. Reputational damage 2. Regulatory action / sanction from ICO*
E.g.	*Staff are not aware of how they will be monitored whilst they are working at home*	*Individuals not aware that their data is being processed / unaware of the new use for their personal data*	*Non-compliance with data protection principles – fair, lawful & transparent processing*	*1. Reputational damage 2. Regulatory action / sanction from ICO*
E.g.	*Confidential waste*	*Confidential information may not be disposed of in a secure manner*	*Non-compliance with data protection principles – integrity & confidentiality*	*1. Reputational damage 2. Regulatory action / sanction from ICO*

E.g.	*Video conferencing technology*	*Personal information may be shared via an unsecure platform*	*Non-compliance with data protection principles – fair, lawful & transparent processing and integrity and confidentiality*	*1. Reputational damage 2. Regulatory action / sanction from ICO*
E.g.	*Confidentiality of information whilst working at home*	*Confidential information may be accessed by other household members*	*Non-compliance with data protection principles – integrity & confidentiality*	*1. Reputational damage 2. Regulatory action / sanction from ICO*
E.g.	*Suspected data breaches are not reported in the usual manner*	*Remedial action cannot be taken to reduce the risk of harm of the breach*	*Non-compliance with data protection principles – integrity & confidentiality and accountability*	*1. Reputational damage 2. Regulatory action / sanction from ICO*

1.4 Identify privacy solutions

Use the below to describe the actions you could take to reduce the risks, and any further steps which may be necessary:

No.	Risk	Solutions(s)	Result: is the risk eliminated, reduced or accepted?	Evaluation: is the final impact compliant and proportionate to the aims of the project after the solutions(s) is implemented?
E.g.	*Remote access could be compromised by malicious third parties (taken from table at 1.3 above)*	*We have introduced a multi-factor authentication for logging onto our system remotely*	*Risk reduced to an acceptable level*	*Yes*
E.g.	*Use of staff personal devices*	*We have implemented a BYOD Policy setting out how staff must access, handle and use information on their own devices*	*Risk reduced to an acceptable level*	*Yes*
E.g.	*Individuals are not aware of the project*	*Communication plan to be developed to ensure compliance with data protection principles. Privacy notices are also to be updated.*	*Risk reduced to an acceptable level*	*Yes*
E.g.	*Confidential information may not be disposed of in a secure manner*	*We have communicated to staff how confidential waste is to be disposed of and relevant policies have been updated.*	*Risk reduced to an acceptable level*	*Yes*

E.g.	*Video conferencing technology*	*We have approved the use of [INSERT] for staff to use for work purposes. Use of any unauthorised platforms or apps are not permitted. Relevant policies have been updated to reflect this.*	*Risk reduced to an acceptable level*	*Yes*
E.g.	*Confidentiality of information whilst working at home*	*Staff have a secure environment to work in at home. Relevant policies have been updated to reiterate the importance of confidentiality whilst out of the office.*	*Risk reduced to an acceptable level*	*Yes*
E.g.	*Suspected data breaches are not reported in the usual manner*	*Communication plan to be developed to ensure compliance with breach reporting obligations. Relevant policies have been updated where necessary.*	*Risk reduced to an acceptable level*	*Yes*

2. Link the DPIA to the Data Protection Principles

Question	Response	Required Action e.g. seek advice from senior member of staff
What is the legal basis for processing the information? *This should refer to the conditions for processing under the GDPR and Data Protection Act 2018*		
How will individuals be told about the use of their personal data?		
Do you need to amend your privacy notices?		
Do you need to amend any existing policies or create new policies/procedures?		
Does the project involve the use of existing personal data for new purposes?		
Are potential new purposes likely to be identified as the scope of the project expands?		

Are you able to amend information when necessary to ensure it is up to date?		
How are you ensuring that personal data obtained from individuals or other organisations is accurate?		
What are the retention periods for the personal information and how will this be implemented?		
Will you be able to easily action requests from individuals for access to their personal information?		
Do any new systems provide protection against the security risks you have identified?		
What training and instructions are necessary to ensure that staff know how to operate a new system secure?		

Will the project require you to transfer data outside of the EEA? (e.g. if any of the technology you are implementing are based in the US)		
If you will be making transfers outside the EEA, how will you ensure that the data is adequately protected?		

3. Sign off and record the DPIA outcomes

Use this section to confirm who has approved the privacy risks involved in the project and what solutions need to be implemented:

Risk	Approved Solutions(s)	Approved by

4. Integrate the DPIA outcomes back into the project plan

Use this section to confirm who is responsible for integrating the DPIA outcomes back into the project plan and update any project management paperwork. Also confirm who is responsible for implementing the solutions that have been approved and provide contact details for any privacy concerns which may arise in the future.

No.	Action to be Taken	Date for Completion of Action	Responsibility for Action

MORE BOOKS BY LAW BRIEF PUBLISHING

A selection of our other titles available now:-

'Covid-19, Force Majeure and Frustration of Contracts – The Essential Guide' by Keith Markham
'Covid-19 and Criminal Law – The Essential Guide' by Ramya Nagesh
'Covid-19 and Family Law in England and Wales – The Essential Guide' by Safda Mahmood
'Covid-19 and the Implications for Planning Law – The Essential Guide' by Bob Mc Geady & Meyric Lewis
'Covid-19, Residential Property, Equity Release and Enfranchisement – The Essential Guide' by Paul Sams and Louise Uphill
'Covid-19, Brexit and the Law of Commercial Leases – The Essential Guide' by Mark Shelton
'Covid-19 and the Law Relating to Food in the UK and Republic of Ireland – The Essential Guide' by Ian Thomas
'A Practical Guide to the General Data Protection Regulation (GDPR) – 2nd Edition' by Keith Markham
'Ellis on Credit Hire – Sixth Edition' by Aidan Ellis & Tim Kevan
'A Practical Guide to Working with Litigants in Person and McKenzie Friends in Family Cases' by Stuart Barlow
'Protecting Unregistered Brands: A Practical Guide to the Law of Passing Off' by Lorna Brazell
'A Practical Guide to Secondary Liability and Joint Enterprise Post-Jogee' by Joanne Cecil & James Mehigan
'A Practical Guide to the Pre-Action RTA Claims Protocol for Personal Injury Lawyers' by Antonia Ford
'A Practical Guide to Neighbour Disputes and the Law' by Alexander Walsh
'A Practical Guide to Forfeiture of Leases' by Mark Shelton

'A Practical Guide to Coercive Control for Legal Practitioners and Victims' by Rachel Horman
'A Practical Guide to Rights Over Airspace and Subsoil' by Daniel Gatty
'Tackling Disclosure in the Criminal Courts – A Practitioner's Guide' by Narita Bahra QC & Don Ramble
'A Practical Guide to the Law of Driverless Cars – Second Edition' by Alex Glassbrook, Emma Northey & Scarlett Milligan
'A Practical Guide to TOLATA Claims' by Greg Williams
'Artificial Intelligence – The Practical Legal Issues' by John Buyers
'A Practical Guide to the Law of Prescription in Scotland' by Andrew Foyle
'A Practical Guide to the Construction and Rectification of Wills and Trust Instruments' by Edward Hewitt
'A Practical Guide to the Law of Bullying and Harassment in the Workplace' by Philip Hyland
'How to Be a Freelance Solicitor: A Practical Guide to the SRA-Regulated Freelance Solicitor Model' by Paul Bennett
'A Practical Guide to Prison Injury Claims' by Malcolm Johnson
'A Practical Guide to the Small Claims Track' by Dominic Bright
'A Practical Guide to Advising Clients at the Police Station' by Colin Stephen McKeown-Beaumont
'A Practical Guide to Antisocial Behaviour Injunctions' by Iain Wightwick
'Practical Mediation: A Guide for Mediators, Advocates, Advisers, Lawyers, and Students in Civil, Commercial, Business, Property, Workplace, and Employment Cases' by Jonathan Dingle with John Sephton
'The Mini-Pupillage Workbook' by David Boyle
'A Practical Guide to Crofting Law' by Brian Inkster
'A Practical Guide to Spousal Maintenance' by Liz Cowell
'A Practical Guide to the Law of Domain Names and Cybersquatting' by Andrew Clemson
'A Practical Guide to the Law of Gender Pay Gap Reporting' by Harini Iyengar
'A Practical Guide to the Rights of Grandparents in Children Proceedings' by Stuart Barlow
'NHS Whistleblowing and the Law' by Joseph England

'Employment Law and the Gig Economy' by Nigel Mackay & Annie Powell

'A Practical Guide to Noise Induced Hearing Loss (NIHL) Claims' by Andrew Mckie, Ian Skeate, Gareth McAloon

'An Introduction to Beauty Negligence Claims – A Practical Guide for the Personal Injury Practitioner' by Greg Almond

'Intercompany Agreements for Transfer Pricing Compliance' by Paul Sutton

'Zen and the Art of Mediation' by Martin Plowman

'A Practical Guide to the SRA Principles, Individual and Law Firm Codes of Conduct 2019 – What Every Law Firm Needs to Know' by Paul Bennett

'A Practical Guide to Adoption for Family Lawyers' by Graham Pegg

'A Practical Guide to Industrial Disease Claims' by Andrew Mckie & Ian Skeate

'A Practical Guide to Redundancy' by Philip Hyland

'A Practical Guide to Vicarious Liability' by Mariel Irvine

'A Practical Guide to Applications for Landlord's Consent and Variation of Leases' by Mark Shelton

'A Practical Guide to Relief from Sanctions Post-Mitchell and Denton' by Peter Causton

'A Practical Guide to Equity Release for Advisors' by Paul Sams

'A Practical Guide to Unlawful Eviction and Harassment' by Stephanie Lovegrove

'A Practical Guide to the Law Relating to Food' by Ian Thomas

'A Practical Guide to Financial Services Claims' by Chris Hegarty

'The Law of Houses in Multiple Occupation: A Practical Guide to HMO Proceedings' by Julian Hunt

'A Practical Guide to Unlawful Eviction and Harassment' by Stephanie Lovegrove

'A Practical Guide to Solicitor and Client Costs' by Robin Dunne

'Occupiers, Highways and Defective Premises Claims: A Practical Guide Post-Jackson – 2nd Edition' by Andrew Mckie

'A Practical Guide to Financial Ombudsman Service Claims' by Adam Temple & Robert Scrivenor

'A Practical Guide to Advising Schools on Employment Law' by Jonathan Holden

'A Practical Guide to Running Housing Disrepair and Cavity Wall Claims: 2nd Edition' by Andrew Mckie & Ian Skeate

'A Practical Guide to Holiday Sickness Claims – 2nd Edition' by Andrew Mckie & Ian Skeate
'Arguments and Tactics for Personal Injury and Clinical Negligence Claims' by Dorian Williams
'A Practical Guide to QOCS and Fundamental Dishonesty' by James Bentley
'A Practical Guide to Drone Law' by Rufus Ballaster, Andrew Firman, Eleanor Clot
'A Practical Guide to Compliance for Personal Injury Firms Working With Claims Management Companies' by Paul Bennett
'A Practical Guide to the Landlord and Tenant Act 1954: Commercial Tenancies' by Richard Hayes & David Sawtell
'A Practical Guide to Dog Law for Owners and Others' by Andrea Pitt
'RTA Allegations of Fraud in a Post-Jackson Era: The Handbook – 2nd Edition' by Andrew Mckie
'RTA Personal Injury Claims: A Practical Guide Post-Jackson' by Andrew Mckie
'On Experts: CPR35 for Lawyers and Experts' by David Boyle
'An Introduction to Personal Injury Law' by David Boyle
'A Practical Guide to Chronic Pain Claims' by Pankaj Madan
'A Practical Guide to Claims Arising from Fatal Accidents' by James Patience
'A Practical Guide to Subtle Brain Injury Claims' by Pankaj Madan

These books and more are available to order online direct from the publisher at www.lawbriefpublishing.com, where you can also read free sample chapters. For any queries, contact us on 0844 587 2383 or mail@lawbriefpublishing.com.

Our books are also usually in stock at www.amazon.co.uk with free next day delivery for Prime members, and at good legal bookshops such as Wildy & Sons.

We are regularly launching new books in our series of practical day-to-day practitioners' guides. Visit our website and join our free newsletter to be kept informed and to receive special offers, free chapters, etc.

You can also follow us on Twitter at www.twitter.com/lawbriefpub.

www.ingramcontent.com/pod-product-compliance
Lightning Source LLC
LaVergne TN
LVHW022045200926
848481LV00003B/798